PowerPoint™
for Windows® 95
Visual Quick Reference

Tracy Lehman Cramer

PowerPoint for Windows 95 Visual Quick Reference

Library of Congress Catalog No.: 95-71434

ISBN: 1-7897-0684-9

97 96 95   6 5 4 3 2 1

Interpretation of the printing code: the rightmost double-digit number is the year of the book's printing; the rightmost single-digit number, the number of the book's printing. For example, a printing code of 95-1 shows that the first printing of the book occurred in 1995.

Screen reproductions in this book were created using Collage Plus from Inner Media, Inc., Hollis, NH.

President   Roland Elgey

Vice President and Publisher   Marie Butler-Knight

Associate Publisher   Don Roche Jr.

To my family who is always there for me, especially when I need them. A special dedication just to my brother Dan, who can never again complain that I forget him in the dedications of my books. Congrats on the engagement, too! Also, to Weeze, Blair Monster, and Sir Giles, my wonderful Canadian friends, who have added a new, rich dimension to my life.

Editorial Services Director
Elizabeth Keaffaber

Managing Editor
Michael Cunningham

Director of Marketing
Lynn E. Zingraf

Senior Series Editor
Chris Nelson

Acquisitions Editor
Deborah F. Abshier

Product Director
Robin Drake

Production Editor
Lori A. Lyons

Assistant Product Marketing Manager
Kim Margolius

Technical Editor
J. David Shinn, CNE

Acquisitions Coordinator
Tracy M. Williams

Operations Coordinator
Patty Brooks

Editorial Assistant
Carmen Phelps

Book Designer
Kim Scott

Cover Designer
Jay Corpus

Production Team
Angela Bannan,
Claudia Bell,
Michael Brummitt,
Heather Butler,
Anne Dickerson,
Jason Hand,
Mike Henry,
John Hulse,
Damon Jordan,
Daryl Kessler,
Bob LaRoche, Bobbi
Satterfield, Michael
Thomas, Scott Tullis
Christine Tyner

Indexer
Ginny Bess

Composed in *Stone Serif* and *MCPdigital* by
Que Corporation.

About the Author

Tracy Lehman Cramer was a graphic designer and computer consultant before becoming a full-time writer. She is the author of *CorelDRAW! 5 VisiRef* and *PageMaker 5 for Windows VisiRef,* and also contributed to Que's *Guide to Lotus Organizer.* Tracy has also written scripts for interactive CD-ROM software tutorials and is currently involved in creating CD-ROMs to be included with other Que books. She lives in Indianapolis with her husband and three adorable children.

Acknowledgments

Thanks to: Deb Abshier for keeping me busy and having faith; Robin Drake, for her insightful input and kind words; Lori Lyons, for her excellent editing skills; Tracy Williams & the bun, just for putting up with me; the production staff, for making this book look great; and finally to my husband, Doug, for first building me a new computer and then fixing my hard drive when it crashed one Sunday morning in October.

Contents

Introduction   **1**

  How To Use This Book 1

**1 Basics: Start, Exit, Open, Save, View,
  AutoContent Wizard**   **3**

  Starting PowerPoint 3
  Using the AutoContent Wizard 4
  Entering Text in Placeholders 7
    To replace one or more words 7
    To replace all the placeholder text 8
  Moving between Slides 9
  Adding a New Slide 10
  Deleting a Slide 11
  Switching Views 12
    To change the view with the View menu 12
    To use the view buttons 12
  Changing the Order of the Slides 13
  Saving a Presentation 14
  Opening an Existing Presentation 15
    To open from the starting dialog box 15
    To open from the menu or toolbar 15
    To select the presentation to open 15
  Starting a New Presentation 16
    To start a new presentation when starting
      PowerPoint 16
    To start a new presentation with PowerPoint open ...17
  Exiting PowerPoint 18

**2 Graphs: Adding, Editing, Formatting, Resizing,
  Deleting**   **19**

  Adding a Graph to a Graph Layout Slide 19
  Adding a Graph to a Slide without a Graph Layout 20
  Using the Datasheet Window 21
    To graph only parts of a datasheet 21
    To use a spreadsheet table in a graph 22

To edit graph data 24
Changing the Graph Type 25
Formatting a Graph 26
   To choose a subtype 26
   To change the depth of the graph 27
   To change the space between columns or bars 28
   To rotate a graph 29
   To change the color scheme 30
   To graph by row or column 32
   To format text in a graph 33
   To format numbers in a graph 34
Resizing a Graph 35
Adding or Removing a Legend .36
Deleting a Graph 37

3 Editing Text: Moving, Copying, AutoCorrect, Bullets, Finding/Replacing   39

Selecting Text 39
Editing Text 40
   To delete a single character .40
   To replace existing text 41
   To insert new text into existing text 42
Moving and Copying Text 43
   To cut text 43
   To copy text 44
   To paste text 45
   To drag and drop text 46
Checking Spelling 47
Using AutoCorrect 48
   To use AutoCorrect as you're typing 48
   To correct a word 48
   To add a word 49
   To delete an entry 49
Checking the Style of Your Presentation 50
Applying Fonts and Text Attributes 52
   To change the font 52
   To change the point size 53
   To apply font styles 54
   To apply multiple attributes .55
Changing Paragraph Alignment 56
Changing the Line Spacing 57

To change the line spacing 57
To change the paragraph spacing 58
Editing Paragraph Bullets 59
Finding and Replacing Text .61
To find text 61
To replace text 62

4 Enhancements: Changing Layout, Background, Format, Color, Adding Animation 65

Editing the Slide Master 65
Selecting a New Layout for a Slide 67
Changing Slide Backgrounds 68
To add a shaded fill 68
To add a patterned fill 70
To add a textured background 71
To add clip art as a background 72
Changing the Slide Format and Orientation 73
Adding Header and Footer Text 74
Adding a footer 74
Adding a date, time, or page number 75
Selecting a New Color Scheme 76
Animating Text 77

5 Handouts and Notes: Add, Edit, Print, Format, Graphics 79

Creating Notes Pages for Slides 79
To make a notes page 79
To change the layout of notes pages 80
To change the master elements for the notes pages . . .82
Creating Handouts 83
Adding Text and Graphics to Handouts and Notes 84
To add a header or footer 84
To add the date 85
To format text in a header or footer 86
To add a graphic 86
Printing Notes Pages and Handouts 88

6 Organization Charts: Create, Edit, Colors, Levels, Style   89

Creating an Organization Chart 89
Editing the Chart 91
Changing the Color of Boxes and Backgrounds 93
   To change the line width 93
   To change the color of boxes 94
   To change the style of a box's border 95
   To change the border color for a box 95
   To add a shadow to boxes 96
   To change the background color 97
Adding Emphasis to Text 98
   To change the text attributes 98
   To change the color of text .99
Changing the Structure on the Organization Chart . . .100
   To add levels 100
   To change the reporting structure 101
   To eliminate positions 102
Changing the Chart's Style 103
Selecting Parts of an Organization Chart 104

7 Outlines: Entries, Demote/Promote, Expand/Collapse, Format   105

Entering Text 105
Moving Entries 106
   To move text with the Move button 106
   To drag and drop an entry 107
Demoting and Promoting Entries 108
   To demote entries 108
   To promote entries 109
Expanding and Collapsing the Outline 110
   To collapse slide entries 110
   To expand slide entries 111
Changing the Formatting of Outline Text 112
   To format a single line 112
   To format multiple lines 113

8 Printing: Print Options, Genigraphics, Black-and-White View   115

Printing a Presentation 115
   To specify the printer settings 116
   To set up the print job 118
   Previewing the Presentation before Printing 119

9 Slide Shows: Builds, Transitions, Timing, Pack & Go Wizard   121

Copying Slides from Another Presentation 121
Creating Builds 122
   To build text only 122
   To build text and graphics .123
Using Transitions 126
Running the Slide Show Manually 127
Setting the Timing To Run a Slide Show
   Automatically 128
Running the Slide Show Continuously 129
Annotating Slides during the Presentation 130
   To use the pen 130
   To change the pen color 131
Creating and Displaying Hidden Slides 131
   To create a hidden slide 131
   To display a hidden slide during a presentation 131
Ending the Slide Show 132
Using the Pack & Go Wizard .132
   To pack a presentation 132

10 Setting User Options: Toolbars, Rulers, Guides, Buttons   137

Displaying and Hiding Toolbars 137
Moving Toolbars 138
Resizing a Floating Toolbar 139
Creating Custom Toolbars 140
Changing the Images on the Toolbar Buttons 142
Displaying the Ruler 143
Displaying Guides 144
Setting Other User Options 145

11 Tables: Adding, Entering and Editing Data, Enhancing   147

Adding a Table to a Slide 147
   To add a table to a table layout slide 147
   To add a table to a slide without
      a table placeholder 149
Entering Data in the Table .150
Editing the Data 151
Enhancing the Appearance of the Table 152
   To apply Table AutoFormat 152
   To format table text 154
   To change cell height and width 155
   To add borders to the table 156
   To change the shading of a table 157

12 Templates: Using Design Templates, Creating New Templates   159

Using Design Templates 159
   To create a new presentation with a template 159
   To apply a new design template 160
Creating a Design Template .161
   To open an existing template 161
   To change the color scheme 163
   To change the slide master 165
   To save the new slide master 166

13 Multimedia: ClipArt, Movies, Sound, Media Player   167

Using ClipArt Images in Slides 167
   Adding clip art to a ClipArt Slide 167
   Adding clip art to any slide 168
   Replacing a clip art image .169
   Using AutoClipArt 170
   Adding an image to the ClipArt Gallery 171
   Recoloring clip art 173
   Cropping clip art images 174
Adding a Movie to a Slide 175
Inserting Sound Files or Music in a Slide 177
   To insert a sound clip (WAV format) 177
   To insert a music clip (MIDI format) 179

To add an audio CD clip 180
Using the Media Player 180
To select part of a clip 180
To repeat the selection continuously 181
To adjust the volume of the media clip 182

14 Drawing: Shapes, Groups, Fills, Shadows, Animating   183

Drawing Objects 183
To draw a specific shape .183
To create a freeform drawing 184
Manipulating Groups of Objects 185
To group objects 185
To stack objects 185
Rotating and Flipping Objects 186
To rotate 90° to the right or left 186
To flip an object 186
Adding Fills and Shadows 187
To add a fill 187
To add a shadow 187
To use a transparent fill 188
Animating Objects 189

Index   191

How To Use This Book

Welcome to a new concept in quick references! Unlike traditional pocket references, which usually pack a lot of text on the page but few, if any, illustrations, the *Visual Quick Reference* series presents much of its "how-to" information in a visual manner.

This reference is task-oriented and categories of tasks are organized alphabetically so that you can find them quickly. Use the different category sections to locate the task you want, follow the screen shots to see each step in the process, and then complete the task yourself.

If you prefer to learn or recall information by being shown how a task is accomplished, Que's *PowerPoint for Windows 95 Visual Quick Reference* is well-matched to your needs. This book is the perfect complement to Windows and its graphical interface; you don't have to read a lot of text to find the reference information you need.

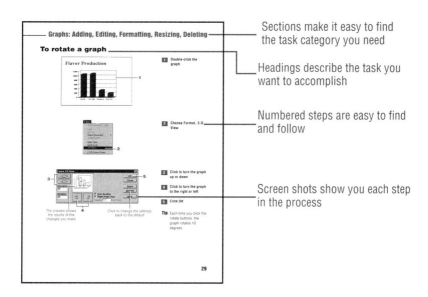

Sections make it easy to find the task category you need

Headings describe the task you want to accomplish

Numbered steps are easy to find and follow

Screen shots show you each step in the process

Starting PowerPoint

When you install PowerPoint (whether as a stand-alone product or with Microsoft Office), the installation program creates a menu shortcut to the PowerPoint program. Rather than starting PowerPoint from the Start menu, you may choose to display the Microsoft Office Shortcut Bar at the top of the screen and just click the PowerPoint button.

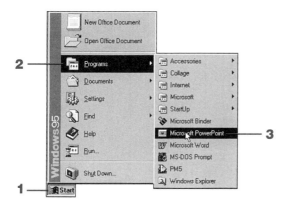

1 Click the Start button

2 Click Programs

3 Click Microsoft PowerPoint

4 Click Next Tip to see another tip (optional)

5 Click OK

Tip Click the Show Tips at Startup check box to deselect the option. Once deselected, no tips will be shown when PowerPoint starts.

Note

Click the More Tips button to move to the Help dialog box and look up more tips on a variety of topics.

Using the AutoContent Wizard

The AutoContent Wizard guides you through the creation of a presentation. You enter information about the type of presentation you want, choose some options, and the Wizard sets up the presentation for you. Each slide has ideas for the content of the slide. Just replace the text on the slide with the information you want.

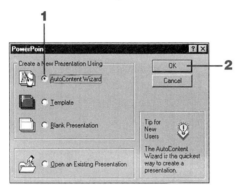

1 Click the AutoContent Wizard option

2 Click OK

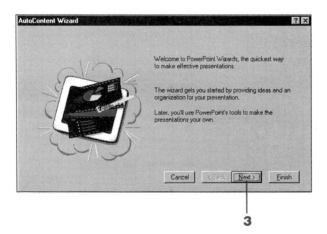

3 Click Next

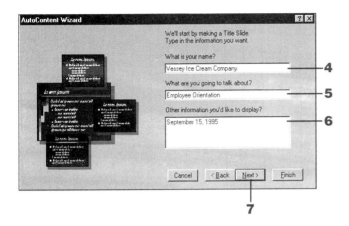

4 Type your name if you want it to appear on the first slide

5 Type the subject of the slide show, if desired

6 Type additional information you want on the first slide, if any

7 Click Next

Tip Click the Back button on the AutoContent Wizard to go back to the previous screen.

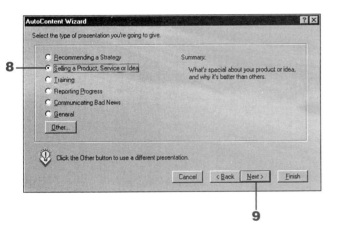

8 Click the option button for the type of presentation you're creating

9 Click Next

Note

Other presentation types are available, but only the six most common are shown on this screen. To pick another type, click the Other button. In the Presentation Template dialog box, select the type of presentation you want from the list and click OK to return to the AutoContent Wizard.

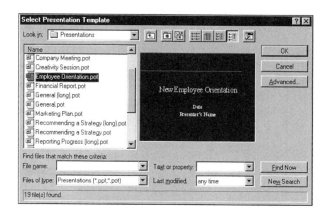

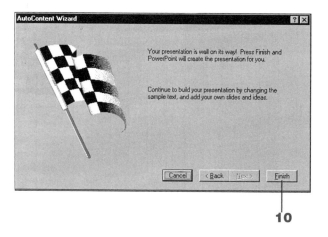

10 Click Finish

10

Entering Text in Placeholders

Each slide has placeholders where the actual text will appear. The placeholders are a dashed-border box with the text "Click to add" inside. When you type new text in the placeholder, the new text is the same typeface and size as the placeholder text was.

To replace one or more words

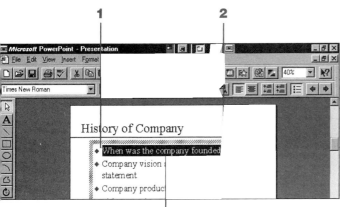

The selected text is highlighted

1 Click and hold the mouse button at the beginning of the text you want to replace

2 Drag over the text

3 Release the mouse button

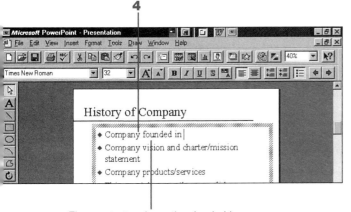

The new text replaces the placeholder

4 Type the new text

7

To replace all the placeholder text

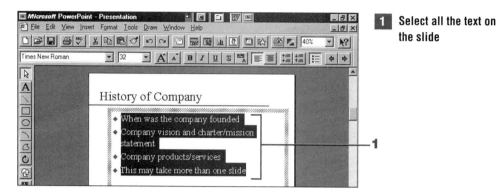

1 Select all the text on the slide

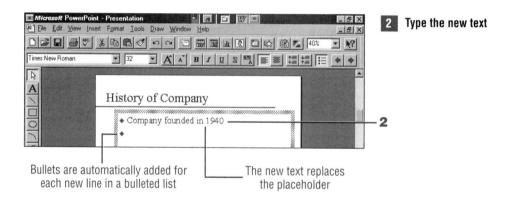

2 Type the new text

Bullets are automatically added for each new line in a bulleted list

The new text replaces the placeholder

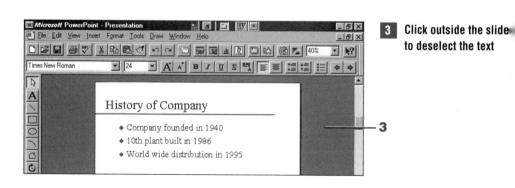

3 Click outside the slide to deselect the text

Moving between Slides

There are several ways you can change to another slide. You'll want to move to different slides to check information, copy and paste text, or check the flow of the slides in the presentation.

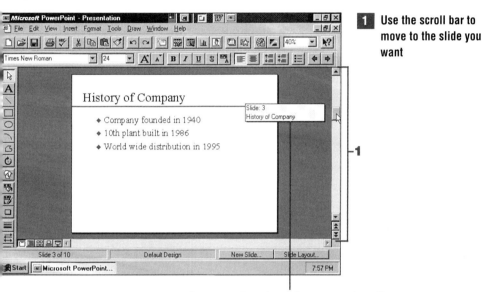

1 Use the scroll bar to move to the slide you want

A message box shows the name and position of the slide that will be displayed

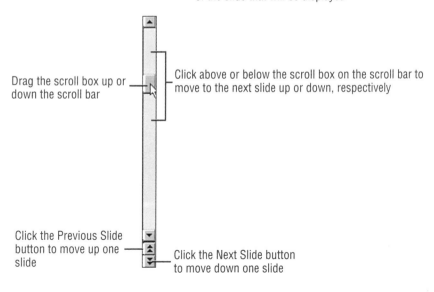

Drag the scroll box up or down the scroll bar

Click above or below the scroll box on the scroll bar to move to the next slide up or down, respectively

Click the Previous Slide button to move up one slide

Click the Next Slide button to move down one slide

9

Adding a New Slide

When you add a new slide, it's inserted after the current slide on the screen. You choose the slide layout to use.

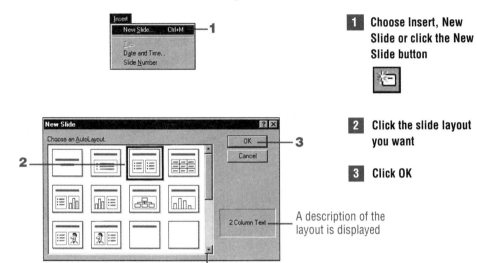

1 Choose Insert, New Slide or click the New Slide button

2 Click the slide layout you want

3 Click OK

A description of the layout is displayed

Scroll down to see more layouts

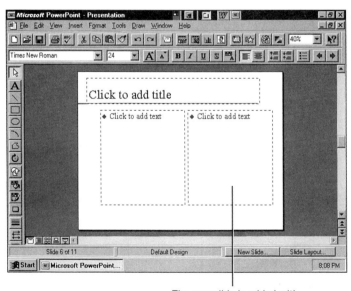

Tip You could add as many slides as the memory on your computer will allow, but it's unlikely you'd want a presentation to be that long.

The new slide is added with placeholders for your text

Deleting a Slide

When you delete a slide, all the information on the slide is also removed.

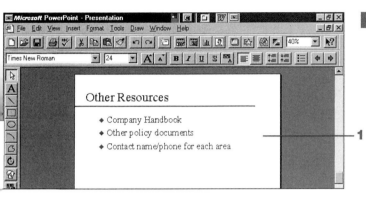

1 Display the slide you want to delete

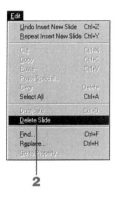

2 Choose Edit, Delete Slide

Tip To bring back a slide you just deleted, choose Edit, Undo before you do anything else. Once you perform another task, the slide is unretrievable.

Note

You must choose Edit, Delete Slide to remove a slide in Slide view; pressing the Delete key does nothing. You can use the Delete key to remove a slide in Outline view if you first select the slide.

Switching Views

Your presentation can be seen in five different views. Slide View shows the slides on-screen one at a time. In Outline View, the text is shown as an outline, and you can't see any clip art, graphs, or tables. Slide Sorter View is used to rearrange the slides, and shows only numbered blank versions of your slides. Use the Notes Pages View to create notes for the speaker about each slide. Choosing Slide Show View runs the presentation.

To change the view with the View menu

1 Choose View

2 Choose the view that you want

To use the view buttons

1 Click the button for the view that you wan

Button	View
🔲	Slide View
📄	Outline View
🔳	Slide Sorter View
🖳	Notes Pages View
🖥	Slide Show

Tip Use the views for different tasks. For editing text on the slides, go to Outline view; change to Slide Sorter view to rearrange the slides. Working solely in Slid view can limit your productivity.

Changing the Order of the Slides

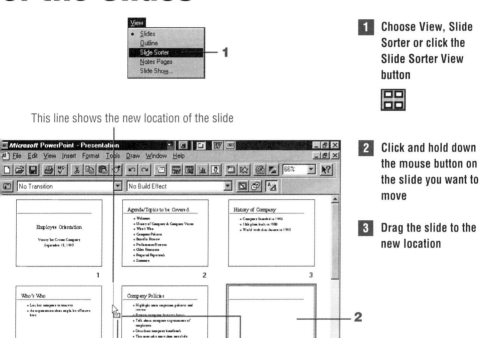

This line shows the new location of the slide

The mouse pointer changes to indicate that you're dragging a slide

1 Choose View, Slide Sorter or click the Slide Sorter View button

2 Click and hold down the mouse button on the slide you want to move

3 Drag the slide to the new location

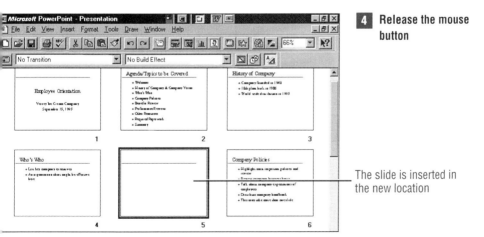

The slide is inserted in the new location

4 Release the mouse button

13

Saving a Presentation

To keep a presentation for further use in the future, you need to save it. You can save it either to the computer's hard disk or to a floppy disk.

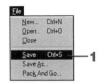

1 Choose File, Save or click the Save button

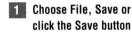

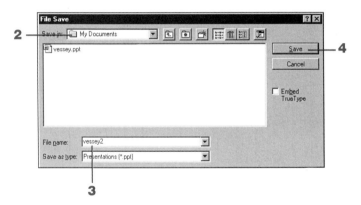

2 Choose the drive and folder in which you want to save the file

3 Type a file name

4 Click Save

Tip You don't need to add the .ppt extension at the end of a file name; PowerPoint will add it for you.

Note

You only have to name a file the first time you save it. The next time you use the Save command, the current file is saved with the same file name, replacing the previous version of the file. You can use the Save As command to save a file under a new name. This is a good idea if you're planning to make many changes but don't know if you'll keep the changes or use the original presentation.

Opening an Existing Presentation

Open an existing presentation to do additional work on it
or to show the slide show. You can open the file from
PowerPoint's starting dialog box, or from the menu or
toolbar. In either case, PowerPoint displays the Open dialog box, where you specify where the file is located.

To open from the starting dialog box

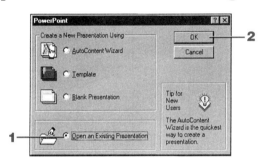

1 Click this option

2 Click OK

To open from the menu or toolbar

1 Choose File, Open or
click the Open button

To select the presentation to open

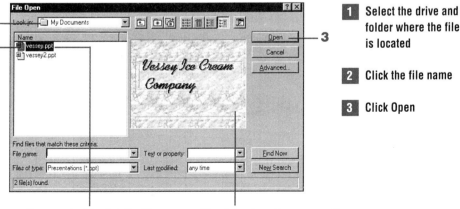

1 Select the drive and
folder where the file
is located

2 Click the file name

3 Click Open

You can double-click the file
name to open the file quickly

The dialog box shows a preview
of the selected presentation

Starting a New Presentation

The AutoContent Wizard sets up a presentation for you, but there may be times when you want to build it by yourself. With a new presentation, you select the type of slide you want for slide 1 and add slides as you go.

To start a new presentation when starting PowerPoint

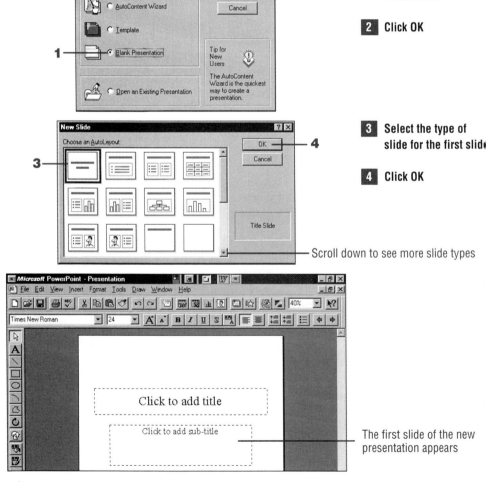

1 Click Blank Presentation

2 Click OK

3 Select the type of slide for the first slide

4 Click OK

Scroll down to see more slide types

The first slide of the new presentation appears

To start a new presentation with PowerPoint open

1 Choose File, New

Tip If you click the New button, the New Slide dialog box appears and you can choose the layout for the first slide.

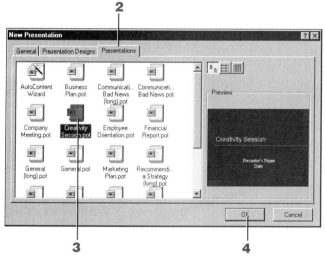

2 Click the Presentations tab, if necessary

3 Click the icon for the presentation style you want

4 Click OK

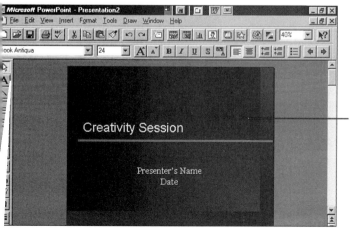

The first slide appears on the page

Note

You can also click the Click To Add First Slide box that appears when no presentations are open.

Exiting PowerPoint

Before you close PowerPoint, remember to save any presentations that are open.

1 Choose File, Exit

Note

If you didn't save the presentation before you chose the Exit command, a message box appears to ask if you want to save the file. Click Yes if you want to save the file or No to exit without saving. Choose Cancel to return to PowerPoint. If you decide to save the file, see the section on Saving a File.

Adding a Graph to a Graph Layout Slide

There are several slide layouts that contain graphs; several also have an area for text. You choose the type from a variety of graphs, including bar, line, and pie graphs. The datasheet, which is similar to an Excel spreadsheet, contains the information for the graph.

Tip Graphs and charts are the same thing. PowerPoint uses the term graph; Excel uses chart.

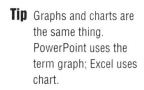

1 Double-click the graph area

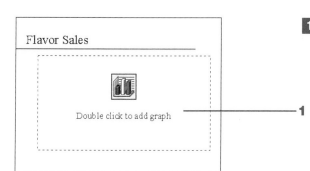

3

2 Select the cell you want to add information to

3 Type the information for the graph in the datasheet window

4 Click the Close button

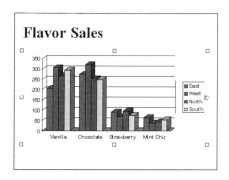

The graph is placed on the slide

19

Adding a Graph to a Slide without a Graph Layout

You don't need to use a graph layout slide to add a graph.
It can be added to a regular slide with text on it as well.
You can change the graph just as you would if it were on a
graph layout slide.

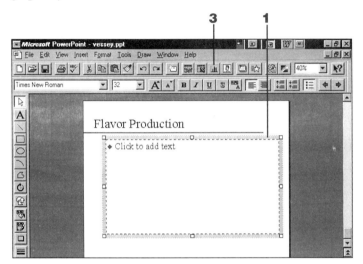

1 Click the text box to select it

2 Press Delete

3 Click the Insert Graph Button

Tip If you want text on the slide with the graph, don't delete the text box. Skip steps 1 and 2, and then resize the text box and the graph box so that they both fit.

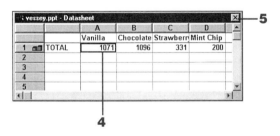

4 Enter the information for the graph in the datasheet window

5 Click the Close button

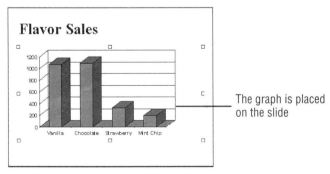

The graph is placed on the slide

Using the Datasheet Window

Graph data is the information that will be plotted on the graph. You enter the data in cells in the datasheet window, with row and column headings to identify the data series. All the data you enter in the datasheet is graphed by default, but you can choose which information to graph and which to exclude. The major difference between this datasheet and an Excel spreadsheet is that you can't add formulas to the datasheet.

Note

A cell is the intersection of a row and column on a spreadsheet; it holds the information you enter.

To graph only parts of a datasheet

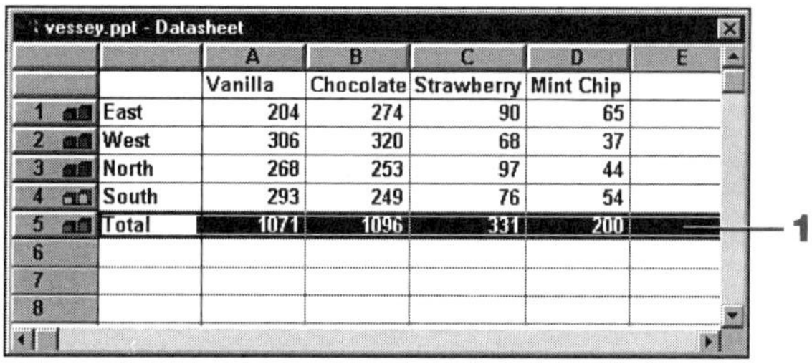

		A	B	C	D	E
		Vanilla	Chocolate	Strawberry	Mint Chip	
1	East	204	274	90	65	
2	West	306	320	68	37	
3	North	268	253	97	44	
4	South	293	249	76	54	
5	Total	1071	1096	331	200	
6						
7						
8						

vessey.ppl - Datasheet

1 Click the heading of the row(s) or column(s) that you don't want to include in the graph

Note

If you want to exclude a column and a row, you have to exclude them individually. You can't select a row and a column at the same time. You can, however, select adjacent rows or columns by holding down the mouse on the first heading and dragging over the other headings you want to select.

21

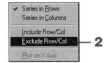

2 Choose Data, Exclude Row/Col

Tip You can also double-click the row or column heading to exclude it. Double-click again to include it.

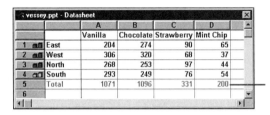

The excluded row is grayed to indicate it won't be graphed

To use a spreadsheet table in a graph

1 Create the table, select it, and copy it to the clipboard

Graphs: Adding, Editing, Formatting, Resizing, Deleting

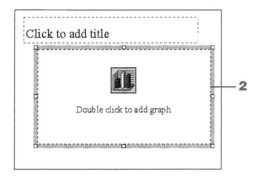

2 Double-click the graph

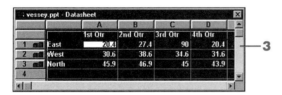

3 Select the entire datasheet

4 Click the right mouse button and choose Clear

5 Click the Paste button

The table is pasted on the datasheet and the information is graphed.

To edit graph data

If you want to change data in the graph, change it in the datasheet window. When you close the datasheet window, the graph is updated.

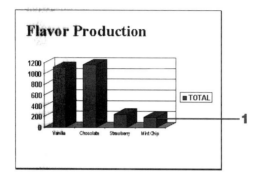

1 Double-click the graph

2 Choose View, Datasheet or click the View Datasheet button

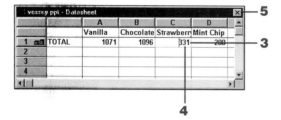

3 Double-click the cell you want to edit

4 Change the data as desired

5 Click the Close button

Changing the Graph Type

You can change the graph to a different type after you've created it. The available types include area, line, pie, and bar graphs, and you can make any of these either two- or three-dimensional. The formatting options vary depending on the type of graph you use.

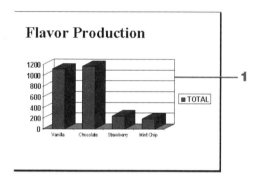

1 Double-click the graph

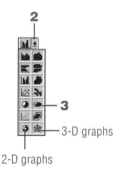

2 Click the drop-down arrow next to the Chart Type button

3 Click the new type of graph

3-D graphs

2-D graphs

Tip The face of the Chart Type button changes to match the type of graph you're currently using. The default version shows a column chart.

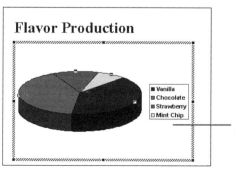

Flavor Production

The graph is changed to the new type

Formatting a Graph

After you enter the data for the graph and place the graph on the slide, it probably won't look exactly the way you want. You can change the colors of the data series as well as the appearance of elements, such as the bars on a bar chart. The formatting choices available depend on the type of chart you're creating.

To choose a subtype

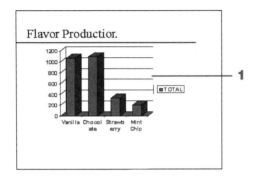

1 Double-click the graph

Tip A subtype is a variation of a chart type. The number of subtypes varies with each kind of chart. There are 3 different types of 3D Bar charts, but only one type of 3-D Pie Chart.

2 Choose Format, then the last item on the menu

The last item shows which type of chart is selected

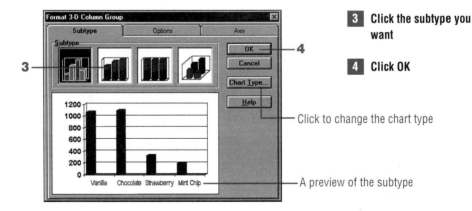

3 Click the subtype you want

4 Click OK

Click to change the chart type

A preview of the subtype

To change the depth of the graph

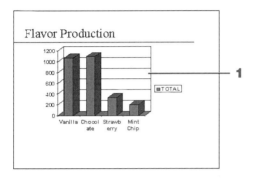

1 Double-click the graph

Tip You can only change the depth of a 3-D graph.

2 Choose Format, then the last item listed on the menu

Increase this to add more room between the data markers

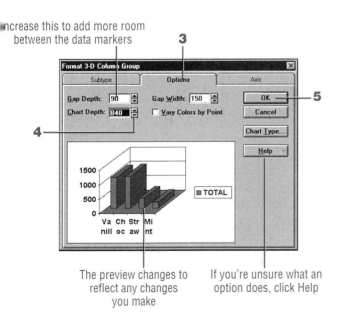

3 Click the Options tab

4 Click the up or down arrows to increase or decrease the depth

5 Click OK

Tip Some labels may overlap in the preview of the chart. You can stretch the chart on the slide to accommodate the labels.

The preview changes to reflect any changes you make

If you're unsure what an option does, click Help

To change the space between columns or bars

Increase the width measurement for a wider gap between the columns. Decrease the measurement to move the columns closer together.

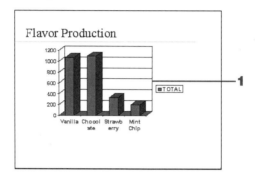

1 Double-click the graph

2 Choose Format, then the last item listed on the menu

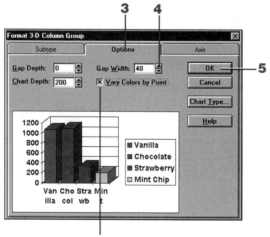

3 Click the Options tab

4 Click the up or down arrow to increase or decrease the gap width

5 Click OK

Click to assign a different color to each data marker in a graph with only one data series

To rotate a graph

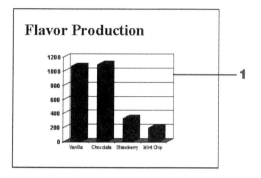

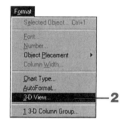

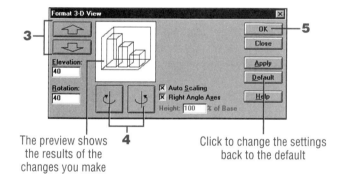

The preview shows
the results of the
changes you make

Click to change the settings
back to the default

1 Double-click the
graph

2 Choose Format, 3-D
View

3 Click to turn the graph
up or down

4 Click to turn the graph
to the right or left

5 Click OK

Tip Each time you click the
rotate buttons, the
graph rotates 10
degrees.

To change the color scheme

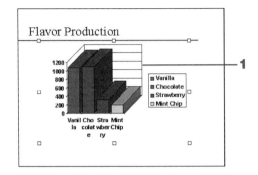

1 Click the graph one time to select it

2 Choose Format, Slide Color Scheme

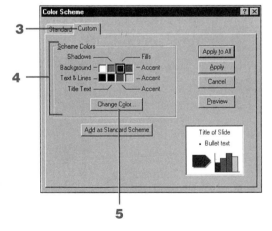

3 Click the Custom tab

4 Click the color box for the element you want to change

5 Click Change Color

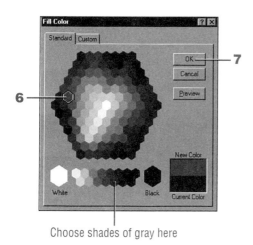

Choose shades of gray here

6 Click the new color you want to use

7 Click OK

Click to apply to all the graphs
in the presentation

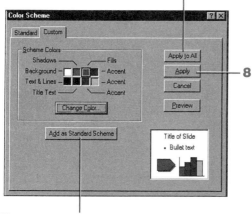

Click to save as a standard scheme

8 Click to apply to only the current slide

Note

If you find a scheme you like, you can save it as a standard
scheme. To apply a standard scheme, click the Standard tab in
the Color Scheme dialog box and click the color scheme you
added.

To graph by row or column

By default, the graph shows the values in the rows of the datasheet. You can change the graph to reflect the values in the columns.

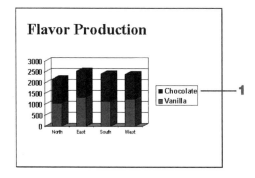

1 Double-click the graph

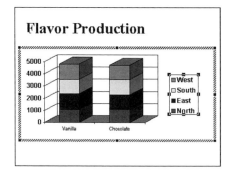

The graph changes to show the values in the selected rows or columns

2 Click the By Rows or By Columns buttons (whichever is appropriate)

To format text in a graph

You can change the text in a graph to any of the fonts, font styles, and sizes on your system to make it easier to read.

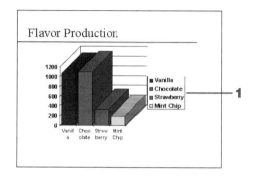

1 Double-click the graph

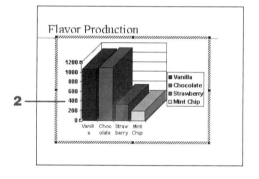

2 Click the text you want to change

Tip When you select text along the x- or y-axis, handles appear on the axis rather than on the text. The formatting changes you make will be applied to the text.

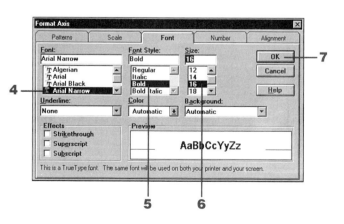

3 Choose Format, Font

4 Select the font

5 Select the font style

6 Select the type size

7 Click OK

To format numbers in a graph

Numbers in a graph appear in the default formatting. You can change the numbers to another format such as currency (with dollar signs, commas, and decimal points rather than plain numbers without separators).

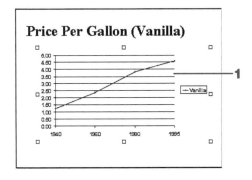

1 Double-click the graph

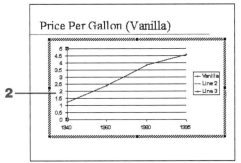

2 Click the numbers you want to format

Number formats are divided into specific categories as well as being displayed in the All category

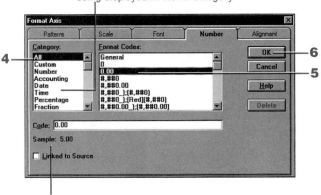

3 Choose Format, Number

4 Select the category of number formats

5 Select the format

6 Click OK

A sample of the selected format is displayed for your review

Resizing a Graph

A chart can be enlarged or reduced by dragging the handles that appear around it when it's selected. You can make the graph only as large as the slide. The text on the graph will be resized as well, so you may also need to change the formatting for that.

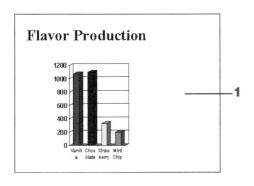

1 Double-click the graph

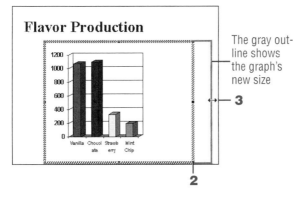

The gray outline shows the graph's new size

2 Click and hold on a handle

3 Drag the handle

4 Release the mouse button

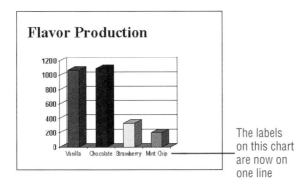

The labels on this chart are now on one line

Adding or Removing a Legend

The legend on a graph shows what each data series represents. You can turn the legend on and off as needed. You
can also format the text as you format text in the graph.

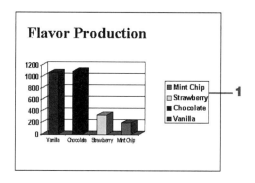

1 Double-click the graph

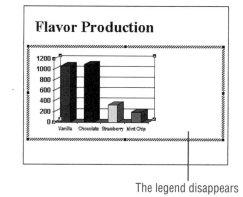

The legend disappears

2 Click the Legend button

Tip To restore the legend, click the Legend but-ton again.

Deleting a Graph

When you delete a graph, it's removed from the presentation. All the data in the datasheet is deleted as well.

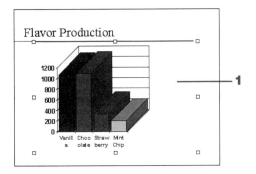

1 Click once on the graph to select it

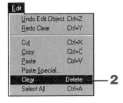

2 Choose Edit, Clear or press the Delete key

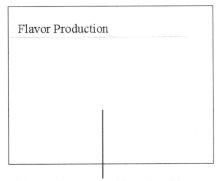

The graph is removed from the slide

Tip Use the Edit, Undo command or click the Undo button immediately after you delete a graph if you want it back.

Selecting Text

Text must be selected before you can make any formatting changes to it, such as enlarging it or changing the font. This is so that PowerPoint knows what element to make the changes to. Selected text is highlighted.

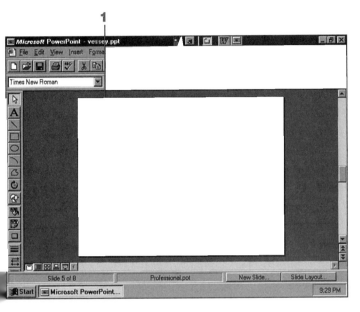

1 Position the cursor in front of the text you want to select

Tip You can also select a single word by double-clicking it, or select an entire sentence by triple-clicking within it.

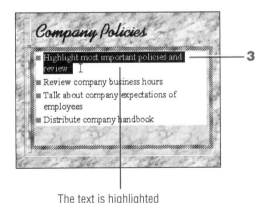

The text is highlighted

2 Press and hold down the mouse button

3 Drag over the text

4 Release the mouse button

Editing Text

Occasionally, you'll need to replace the text you typed with other text—such as when you make a mistake. If you make a simple one-character mistake, it's easiest to use the Backspace or Delete key. To replace a large amount of text like a sentence, select the text and type over it.

To delete a single character

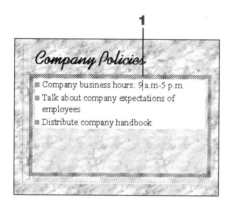

1 Position the insertion point to the right of the character

The character to the left is deleted

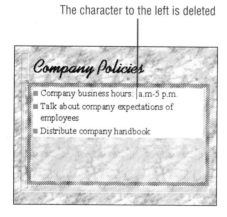

2 Press the Backspace key

Tip You can also delete a character by positioning the insertion point to the left of the character and pressing the Delete key.

To replace existing text

1 Select the text to be replaced

— 1

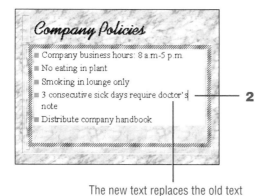

2 Type the new text

— 2

The new text replaces the old text

Note

you work with a word processor, you might be used to
hanging to the Overstrike mode to replace text. PowerPoint,
owever, doesn't recognize the Overstrike mode.

To insert new text into existing text

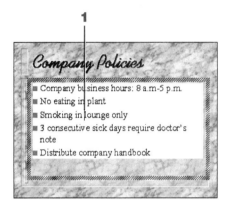

1 Click the insertion point inside the text

The old text makes room for the new

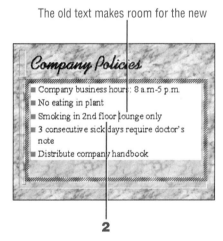

2 Type the new text

Moving and Copying Text

Use the Cut and Copy commands to move text around in your presentation rather than deleting text and then retyping it. The drag-and-drop command is useful for quickly moving text in a few simple steps.

To cut text

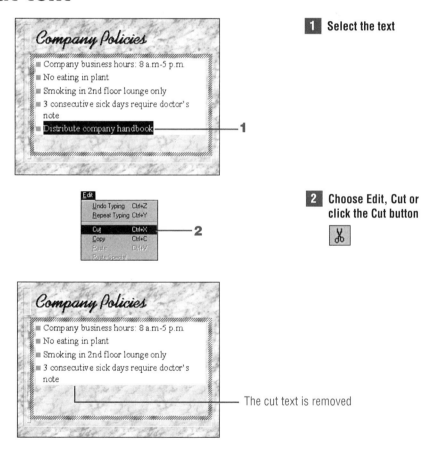

1 Select the text

2 Choose Edit, Cut or click the Cut button

The cut text is removed

Note

A cut or copied item is placed temporarily in the Windows Clipboard. When you cut or copy another item, it replaces the first thing you cut or copied, and the first item is gone. If you think you'll need something you moved to the Clipboard again, you can save it as a clipboard file.

To copy text

1 Select the text

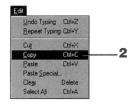

2 Choose Edit, Copy or click the Copy button

Note

The three common editing commands—Cut, Copy, and Paste—can be found on the shortcut menu. To display the shortcut menu, click the right mouse button in the slide window. Don't forget to select the text first if you're cutting or copying.

44

To paste text

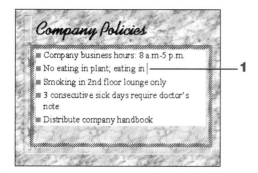

1 Click the insertion point where you want to paste the text

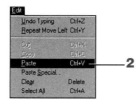

2 Choose Edit, Paste or click the Paste button

The text is placed where the insertion point was located

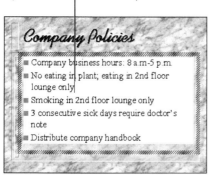

To drag and drop text

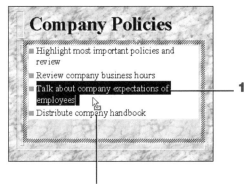

The pointer changes to indicate that you're dragging the text

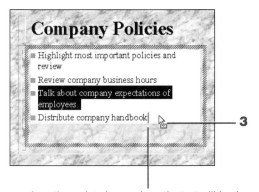

The gray insertion point shows where the text will be dropped

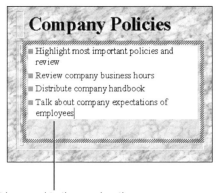

The text is moved to the new location

1 Select the text you want to move

2 Click and hold on the text

3 Drag the text to the new location

4 Release the mouse button

Checking Spelling

The spell checker goes through the entire slide show to check the spelling regardless of what slide you start on. It's likely to find words that aren't really misspelled because the dictionary contains only common English words.

1 Choose Tools, Spelling or click the Spelling button

The spell checker stops at the first misspelled word and highlights it

Click Ignore to ignore the word and find the next

2

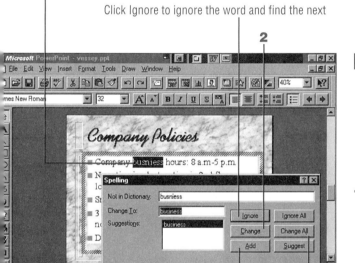

2 If the word in the Change To text box is the correct spelling, click Change

Tip Add your business name (or personal name) to the dictionary so that the spell checker recognizes it.

Click Change All to change all occurrences of the misspelled word to the right spelling

Click Add to add the highlighted word to the dictionary

3 Click OK

Using AutoCorrect

AutoCorrect finds common misspellings of certain words and corrects them as you type. You can add your own words to AutoCorrect and delete words from the predefined list as well.

To use AutoCorrect as you're typing

1 Choose Tools, AutoCorrect

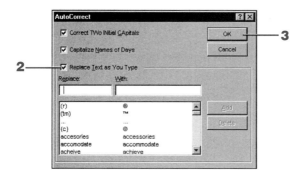

2 Make sure the Replace Text As You Type check box is selected

3 Click OK

To correct a word

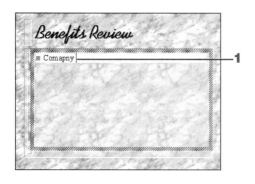

1 Type the word

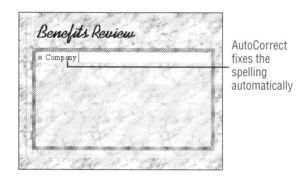

AutoCorrect
fixes the
spelling
automatically

To add a word

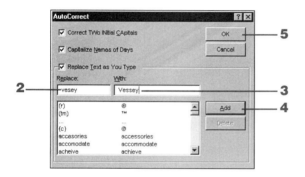

1 Choose Tools,
AutoCorrect

2 Type the misspelling
of the word here

3 Type the correct
spelling here

4 Click Add

5 Click OK

To delete an entry

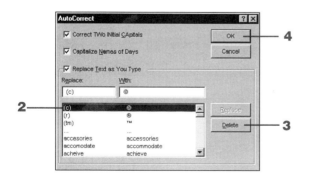

1 Choose Tools,
AutoCorrect

2 Click the entry you
want to delete

3 Click Delete

4 Click OK

49

Checking the Style of Your Presentation

The Style Checker checks your presentation for visual clarity and consistency to make sure all the slides have a uniform appearance. You can choose to have it check your spelling at the same time.

1 Choose Tools, Style Checker

2 Click the options you want to check for

3 Click Start

The Style Checker checks each slide

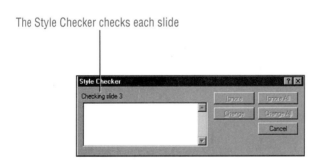

Editing Text: Moving, Copying, AutoCorrect, Bullets

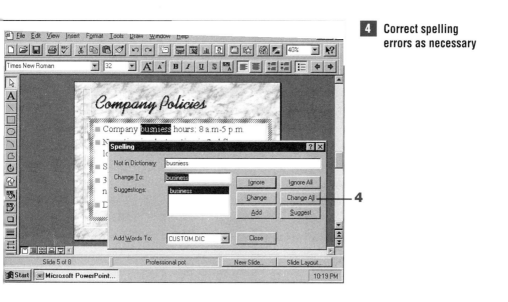

4 Correct spelling
errors as necessary

Here's an explanation of the
error that was found

Click Ignore to ignore the error
and move to the next slide

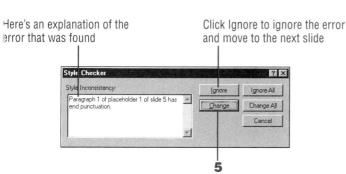

5 If desired, click
Change to change the
error to follow the
styles suggested

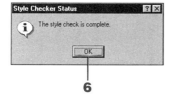

6 Click OK

Applying Fonts and Text Attributes

Use different fonts in your presentation to make it attractive and appealing. The variety of fonts available depends on what is installed on your system. Adding attributes, such as italic, gives the fonts more versatility.

To change the font

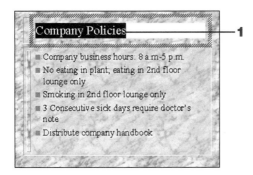

1 Select the text

2 Click the Font box drop-down arrow

3 Click the new font to apply

The font is changed

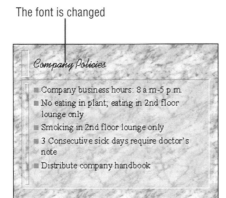

To change the point size

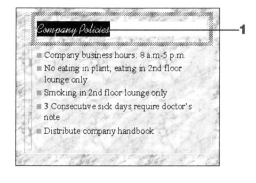

1 Select the text

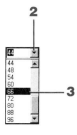

2 Click the Size box drop-down arrow

3 Click the new size to apply

The text size is changed

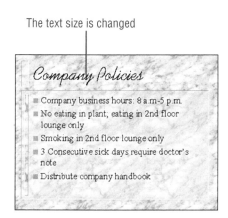

To apply font styles

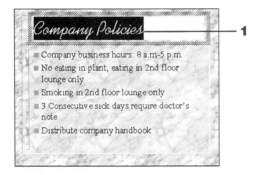

1 Select the text

2 Click the button for the style you want

The text style is changed

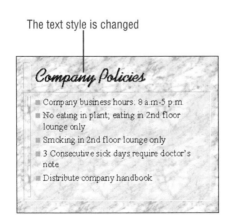

Tip It's easy to go overboard with a lot of type fonts and styles, but the standard rule is to use no more than three different fonts. Even better is to use only two fonts, such as Arial and Times New Roman, and add styles such as bold or italic for variety and emphasis.

To apply multiple attributes

1 Select the text

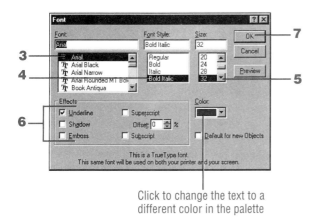

Click to change the text to a
different color in the palette

2 Choose Format, Font

3 Select the font

4 Select the style

5 Select the size

6 Choose any effects to
add

7 Click OK

The text is changed to
the new settings

Changing Paragraph Alignment

The alignment of text refers to the way it's spaced between margins. Left-aligned text is flush on the left margin with an uneven right side, while right-aligned text is flush on the right margin with an uneven left side. Centered text is obviously centered between the margins, and justified text is flush against both margins, with the text spread out evenly between.

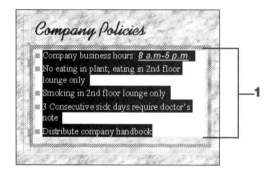

1 Select the text

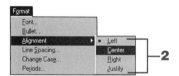

2 Choose Format, Alignment, and the alignment you want, or click the Left Alignment or Center Alignment button

Changing the Line Spacing

If you have only a few items in a bulleted list, you may want to space them out to take up more of the allotted space. Change the paragraph spacing when items take up two or more lines, to add space between the bulleted items but not between the lines for each item.

To change the line spacing

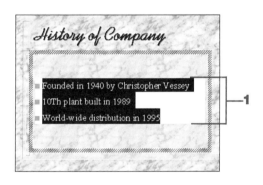

1 Select the text

2 Choose Format, Line Spacing

3 Click the up or down arrow to increase or decrease spacing, or click in the box and type the desired spacing measurement

4 Click OK

57

To change the paragraph spacing

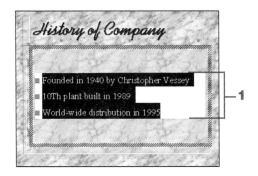

1 Select the paragraphs

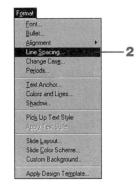

2 Choose Format, Line Spacing

Tip To increase the paragraph spacing by 1, click the Increase Paragraph Spacing button. To decrease the spacing by 1, click the Decrease Paragraph Spacing button.

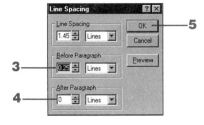

3 Click the up or down arrow to increase or decrease spacing above the paragraph, or click in the box and type the new measurement

4 Click the up or down arrow to increase or decrease spacing below the paragraph, or click in the box and type the new measurement

5 Click OK

Editing Paragraph Bullets

Each presentation uses a specific style of bullet, but if you don't like it, you can choose the bullet to use. Turn off the bullet option if you don't want bullets in the list at all.

1 Select the paragraphs that contain the bullets

2 Choose Format, Bullet

59

Deselect this option if you don't want to use a bullet

Click to change the bullet to a
different color in the palette

Set the size of the
bullet here

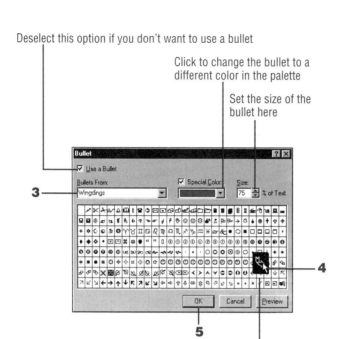

3 Select the font the
new bullet will use

4 Click on the new
bullet style

5 Click OK

The bullet is magnified
so you can see it clearly

The bullets are changed to the new settings

Finding and Replacing Text

The Find feature looks through the entire presentation for the word(s) or phrase you specify. To change that text to something else, use the Replace feature. This finds the text you're looking for and replaces it with the new text.

To find text

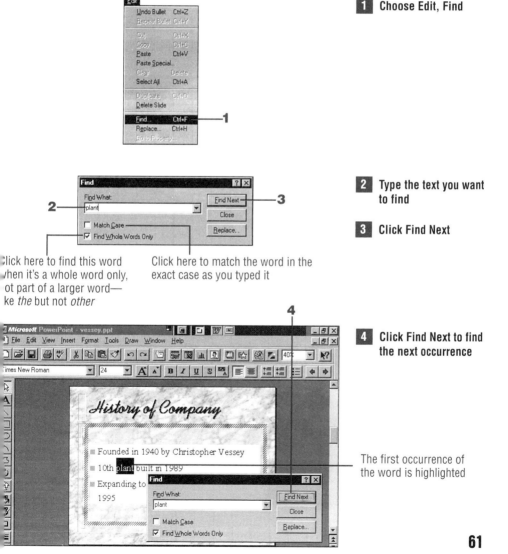

1 Choose Edit, Find

2 Type the text you want to find

3 Click Find Next

Click here to find this word when it's a whole word only, not part of a larger word— like *the* but not *other*

Click here to match the word in the exact case as you typed it

4 Click Find Next to find the next occurrence

The first occurrence of the word is highlighted

61

To replace text

1 Choose Edit, Replace

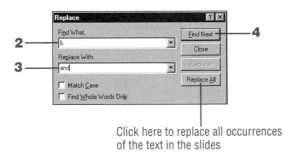

Click here to replace all occurrences
of the text in the slides

2 Type the text to find

3 Type the replacement
text

4 Click Find Next to find
the first occurrence of
the text

The first occurrence of the found text **5**

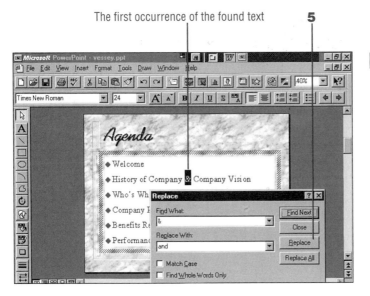

5 Click here to change
the found text and
move to the next
occurrence

The replacement text is inserted

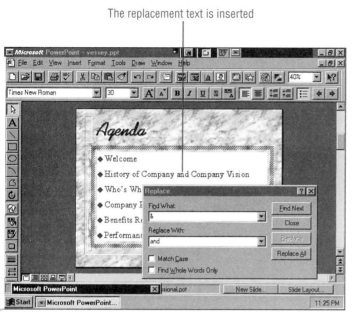

6 Click OK

Editing the Slide Master

The slide master contains all the items that appear on all the slides in a presentation, except the title slide. These items might include a line under the slide title, for example. The font, size, and style are set for each slide on the master as well, even though you can customize the formatting on each individual slide.

1 Choose View, Master, Slide Master

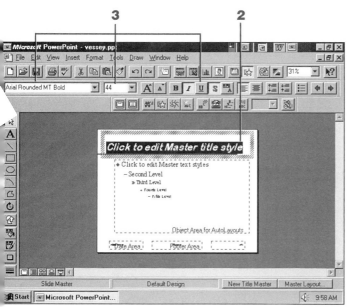

2 Select the item you want to change

3 Apply the desired formatting changes

A slide in the presentation reflects the changes made on the master slide

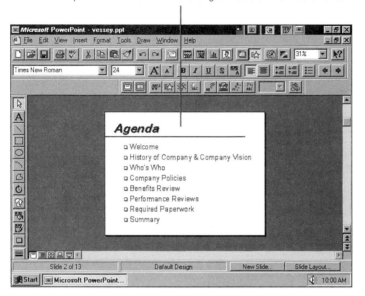

Note

In this example, I'm changing the text attributes, but you can also change many other items on the Slide Master. Just remember: if it appears on all the slides in the presentation, edit the item on the Slide Master.

Selecting a New Layout for a Slide

You can change the layout of a slide at any time. If you decide you don't want the slide to have just a bulleted list of text, but also want a piece of clip art, you can select that type of layout rather than resize the text box and add the clip art yourself.

1 Choose Format, Slide Layout

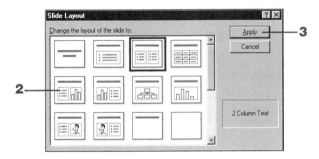

2 Click the type of layout you want

3 Click Apply

The slide layout is changed to the new selection

Tip You can also click the Slide Layout button at the bottom of the PowerPoint screen.

Slide Layout...

67

Changing Slide Backgrounds

If you're planning to show the slide show on a computer, take advantage of the many options for the background of your slides to add to the design of the presentation.

To add a shaded fill

1 Choose Format, Custom Background

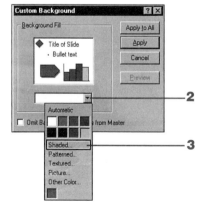

2 Click the drop-down arrow for the back-ground color box

3 Click Shaded on the drop-down menu

Slide this scroll box to make the fill darker or lighter

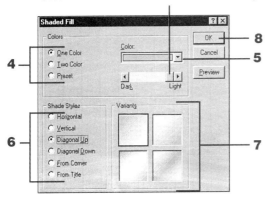

4 Select the type of shaded fill you want

5 Select the color for the fill

6 Select the shade style

7 Click a variation of the shade style, if desired

8 Click OK

Note

There are many preset shaded fills that you can choose from if you don't know what you want for a background. You can also use a preset shade to get an idea for a shaded fill you create.

Click Apply to All to apply to every slide in the presentation

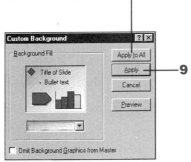

9 Click Apply

To add a patterned fill

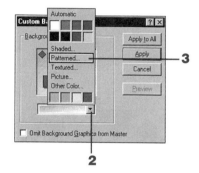

1 To access the Custom Background dialog box, choose Format, Custom Background

2 Click the drop-down arrow for the background color box

3 Choose Patterned

4 Click the pattern for the fill

5 Select the primary color for the pattern

6 Select the background color if you want it to be a color other than white

7 Click OK

8 Click Apply

70

To add a textured background

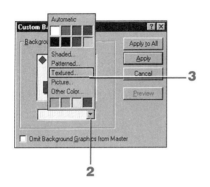

1 To access the Custom Background dialog box, choose Format, Custom Background

2 Click the drop-down arrow for the background color box

3 Choose Textured

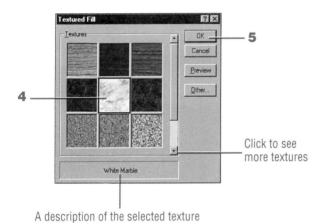

Click to see more textures

A description of the selected texture

4 Click the texture you want

5 Click OK

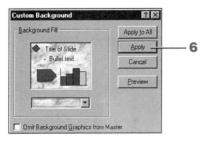

6 Click Apply

To add clip art as a background

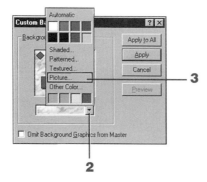

2

3

1 To access the Custom Background dialog box, choose Format, Custom Background

2 Click the drop-down arrow for the background color box

3 Choose Picture

4 5

6

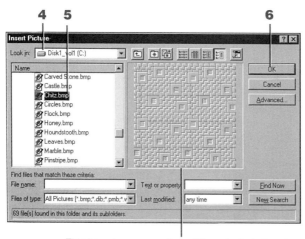

This box shows a preview of the selected clip art

4 Select the drive and folder where the clip art is located

5 Choose the name of the clip art image you want to add

6 Click OK

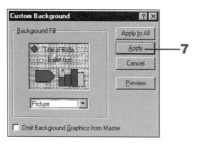

7

7 Click Apply

Changing the Slide Format and Orientation

Each presentation you create is automatically set to be shown on the computer. You can choose to print the presentation on paper or even as 35mm slides. You can also change the slides to portrait orientation (long side vertical) instead of the default landscape orientation (long side horizontal).

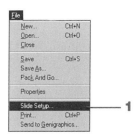

1 Choose File, Slide Setup

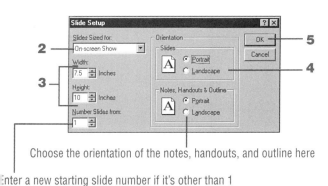

2 Indicate the way you want the slides set up

3 Change the size of the slides, if necessary

4 Choose the orientation of the slides

Choose the orientation of the notes, handouts, and outline here

5 Click OK

Enter a new starting slide number if it's other than 1

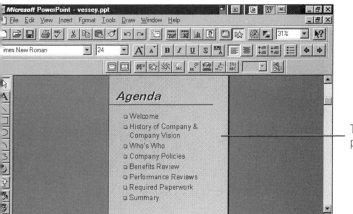

This slide is shown in portrait orientation

73

Adding Header and Footer Text

Header and footer text can be used to identify who created the slides, the name and date of the presentation, and so on. A header appears at the top of the slides; a footer appears at the bottom.

Adding a footer

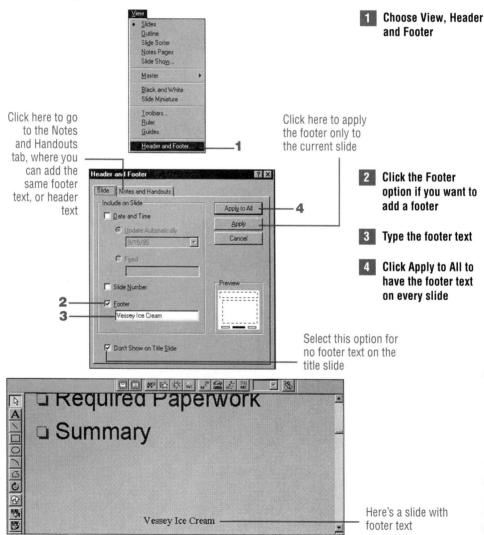

1. Choose View, Header and Footer

Click here to go to the Notes and Handouts tab, where you can add the same footer text, or header text

Click here to apply the footer only to the current slide

2. Click the Footer option if you want to add a footer

3. Type the footer text

4. Click Apply to All to have the footer text on every slide

Select this option for no footer text on the title slide

Here's a slide with footer text

Adding a date, time, or page number

If you add the date or time, you can either add a fixed date that remains the same every time you open the presentation file, or a date field that is updated each time you open the file. Each slide is automatically given the correct number when you choose the number option.

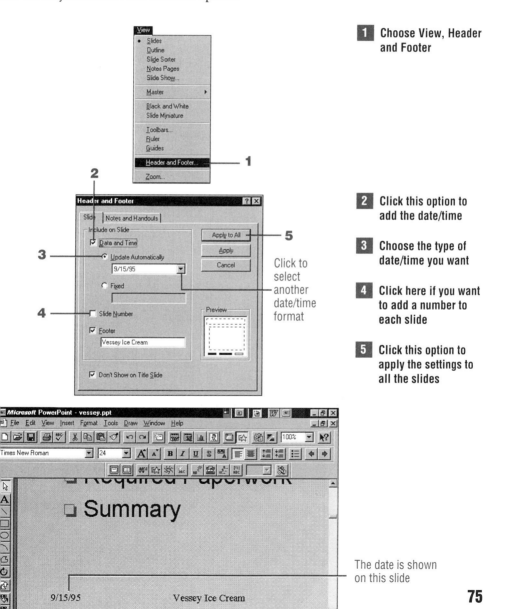

1 Choose View, Header and Footer

2 Click this option to add the date/time

3 Choose the type of date/time you want

Click to select another date/time format

4 Click here if you want to add a number to each slide

5 Click this option to apply the settings to all the slides

The date is shown on this slide

Selecting a New Color Scheme

By choosing a new color scheme for your presentation, you can change the colors of all key elements at one time. If you don't like the color schemes available, you can also create your own.

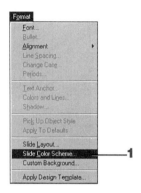

1 Choose Format, Slide Color Scheme

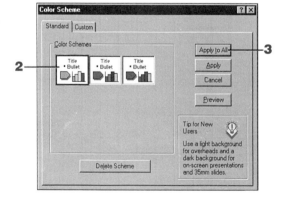

2 Click the new color scheme you want

3 Click Apply to All to add the scheme to every slide

Animating Text

Animated text adds a lot to your presentation because it makes it more interesting than text that just appears on-screen when the slide changes. There are a variety of animation choices that you can combine for an exciting show.

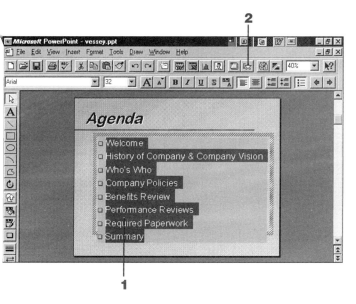

1 Select the text to animate

2 Click the Animation Effects button

Click this to have the presentation build each bit of text automatically, without waiting for you to click the mouse

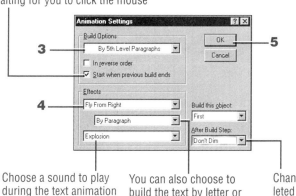

3 Select the way you want to build the text

4 Choose the animation effect for the text

5 Click OK

Choose a sound to play during the text animation for extra emphasis

You can also choose to build the text by letter or word, but each option can get confusing with a large amount of text

Change this to Dim if you want each bulleted item to dim when the next item appears

77

Note

When you have several levels in the text you're animating, you have to decide how to animate each level. If you choose to animate by 5th level paragraphs, one point appears at a time. If you build the text by 2nd level headings, all 3rd, 4th and 5th levels appear as a group.

Creating Notes Pages for Slides

Each notes page contains a small copy of the slide and an area for the presenter to type notes. Each slide has its own notes page, and you can print any or all of them to use as a guide during the presentation.

To make a notes page

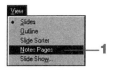

1 Choose View, Notes Pages; or click the Notes Pages View button at the bottom of the screen

To increase the size of the page so you can see what you're typing, click the Zoom Control drop-down arrow and choose another zoom setting

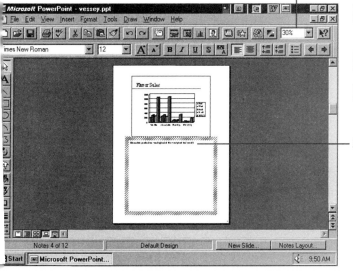

2 Click in the notes body area

3 Type the notes

4 Click the Slide view button or choose View, Slides

To change the layout of notes pages

You may want to change the layout of a notes page so that you have more room to type lengthy notes. Or you might want the slide miniature to be bigger than the default so that you can see tiny details to point out to your audience. The notes page for each slide can be changed to your liking.

1 Choose View, Master, Notes Master or press Shift and click the Notes Pages View button

Tip When you change the layout of the Notes Master, the layout of all the notes pages is changed.

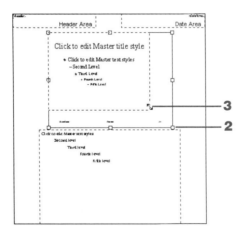

2 Click and hold on a handle

3 Drag to resize the slide

4 Release the mouse button

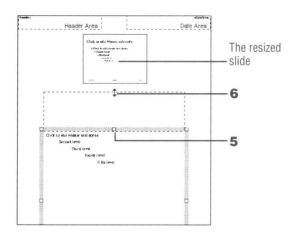

The resized slide

5 Click and hold on a handle

6 Drag to resize the notes box

7 Release the mouse button

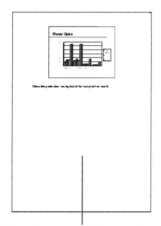

The notes page with the new layout

Note

You can also move the slide and the note box on the page. Click and hold inside the slide or click and hold on the frame of the note box. Drag the object to the new location. This is helpful if you resize an object and want to move it off center so that you have room for notes.

To change the master elements for the notes pages

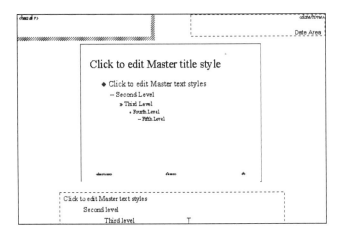

1 Click the element you want to change

Note

If you double-click the slide on the notes page, you move to the slide master, where you can make formatting changes for all the slides.

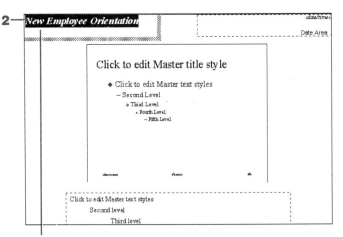

2 Type the information, such as a header

The text you type replaces the text placeholder

You can apply font attributes to this text by using the options on the formatting toolbar or by choosing Format, Font

Creating Handouts

You can print handouts that contain several slides on each page for your presentation audience. Each handout page can have two, three, or six slides on it. If each handout isn't full of slides, you can add text by using the Text tool on the Drawing toolbar.

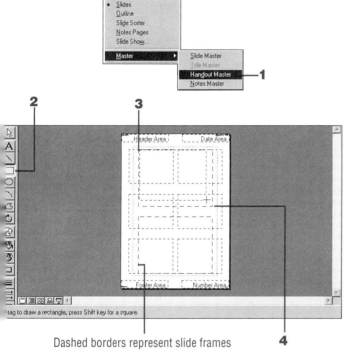

Dashed borders represent slide frames

The handouts for this presentation will have two slides per page

1 Choose View, Master, Handout Master

2 Click the Rectangle Tool button

3 Click and hold at the top corner of the box you want a slide to appear in

4 Drag to the opposite corner to create a frame

5 Repeat the steps for additional slides

Tip You may have to change the fill and line width for the box after you draw it because the Rectangle tool may be set for a certain color and line width.

Adding Text and Graphics to Handouts and Notes

A header or footer with information such as a title can be added to handouts or notes. You can also add the date of the presentation and graphics. The text in the header, footer, and date boxes can be formatted in the font, size, and style you want.

To add a header or footer

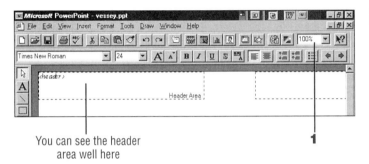

You can see the header
area well here

1 Use the Zoom Contro▮
box to change the
view, if necessary

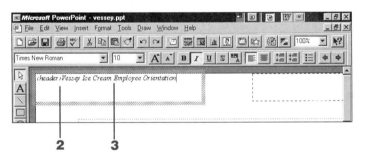

2 Click inside Header
Area or Footer Area
box

3 Type the header or
footer text as desire▮

Tip Resize the box to ma▮
room for more text, i▮
necessary.

4 Click outside the
Header Area or Foo▮
Area box to deselec▮

To add the date

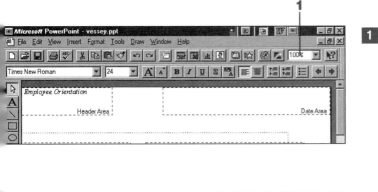

1 Increase the zoom level, if necessary, so you can see what you're doing

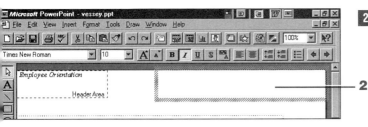

2 Click in the Date Area box

3 Choose Insert, Date and Time

4 Click the date format you want

5 Click OK

Click here to have the date updated each time you open the file

85

To format text in a header or footer

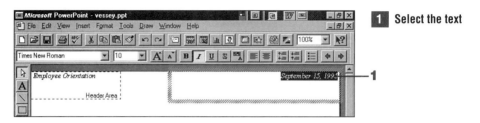

1 Select the text

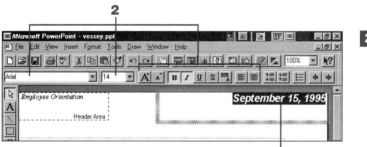

2 Change the font, size or attributes with the toolbar (you can use the Format menu, if you prefer)

The text is changed to the new format

To add a graphic

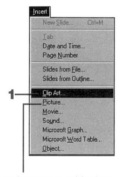

1 Choose Insert, Clip Art

Tip A message may appea at this point asking you to choose any clip art packages you wan added to the gallery. Select the package an click OK.

Click here to insert a graphic that isn't in the clip art library

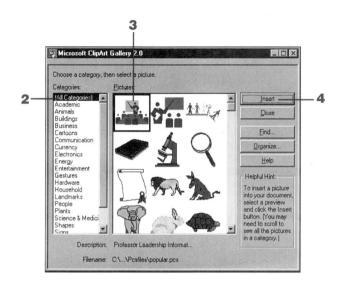

2 Select the category of clip art

3 Click on the picture you want

4 Click Insert

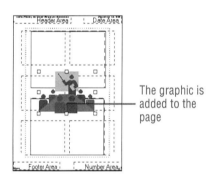

The graphic is added to the page

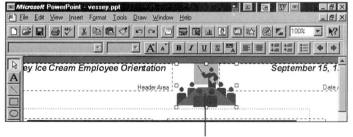

Resize the graphic and move it to the location you want.

Printing Notes Pages and Handouts

You'll want to print copies of the notes pages for yourself and copies of the handouts for your audience. You can select a specific range of pages or print all the pages in the presentation.

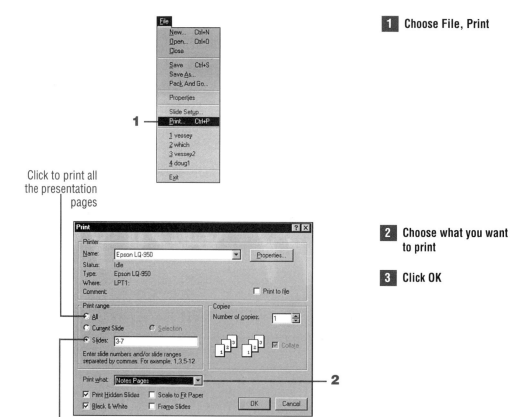

Click to print all
the presentation
pages

Enter a page range here

1 Choose File, Print

2 Choose what you want
to print

3 Click OK

Creating an Organization Chart

An organization chart is used to show the relationships of employees in a company or organization. The application to create organization charts is separate from PowerPoint and starts when you double-click the organization chart placeholder in a slide.

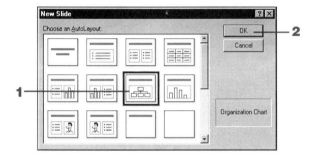

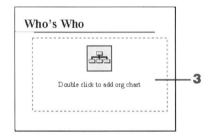

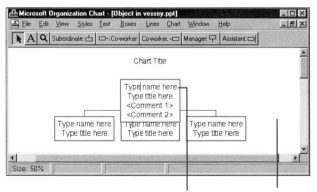

1 Choose the organiza-tion chart layout for a new slide

2 Click OK

Tip You can also insert a new organization chart by choosing Insert, Object, MS Organiza-tion Chart 2.0.

3 Double-click the chart placeholder

Tip If you get an error message that the Organization Chart application can't run, you'll need to go back to the Office Setup program and install the application.

4 Type the first name and title in this box

The Organization Chart application's window appears in PowerPoint

89

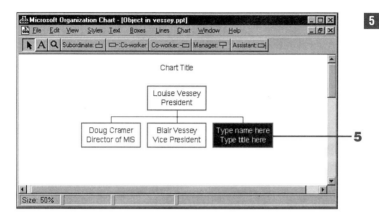

5 Click on each of the boxes you want to add information to and type the information as needed

Note

If you don't want to add a title, select the "Type title here" line and press Delete. No title will appear, but the name and any comments you add will.

6 Choose File, Exit and Return to <*the presentation's file name will appear here*>

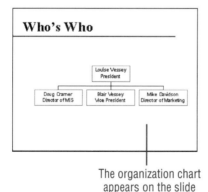

The organization chart appears on the slide

Tip If you Click the Close button, a message appears asking if you want to update the organization chart in your presentation. Click Yes to place the chart on the current slide.

Editing the Chart

You can make changes to the information on an organization chart just as you would any other embedded object. When you double-click the chart on the slide, the Organization Chart application starts in its own window.

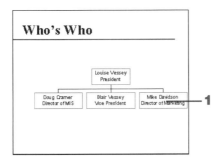

1 Double-click the organization chart on the slide

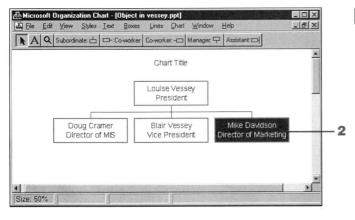

2 Click once on the box you want to edit

Note

When a box is blacked out, it has been selected for the editing of its text contents or to have another box attached to it.

Note

You can quickly select all the boxes in an organizational chart by pressing Ctrl+A.

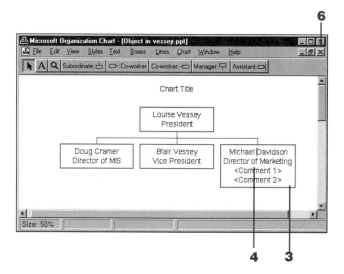

3 Click a second time on the box to add an insertion point

4 Make the desired changes

5 Click outside the box or click another box to make more changes

6 Click the Close button when you finish

Note

Don't double-click the box you want to edit. Double-clicking on a box selects the entire row of boxes.

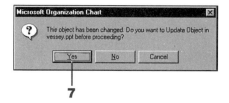

7 Click Yes

Changing the Color of Boxes and Backgrounds

All elements of the organization chart can be changed, like elements on the slide, so the chart is easy to read and attractive.

To change the line width

You can change the width of lines on the chart to make them more visible.

These are the lines you're
changing the width of

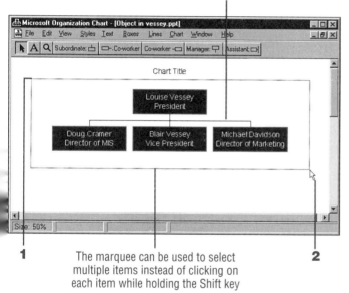

1 Click and hold the mouse button at the top left corner of the area you want to select

2 Drag the pointer to the bottom right corner of the area

3 Release the mouse button

1

The marquee can be used to select multiple items instead of clicking on each item while holding the Shift key

2

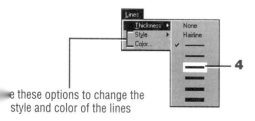

4 Choose Lines, Thickness, and the thickness you want for the lines

e these options to change the style and color of the lines

To change the color of boxes

By default the boxes are blue, which makes the black text difficult to read. If you choose a different color for the background, consider changing the color of the text as well for maximum visibility.

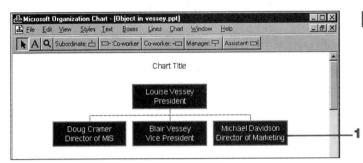

1 Select the box(es) to change

2 Choose Boxes, Color

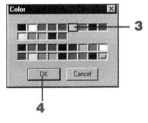

3 Click on the color you want for the boxes

4 Click OK

Note

You don't have the wide selection of colors for an organization chart that you do in PowerPoint, so be careful to choose colors that look good together.

To change the style of a box's border

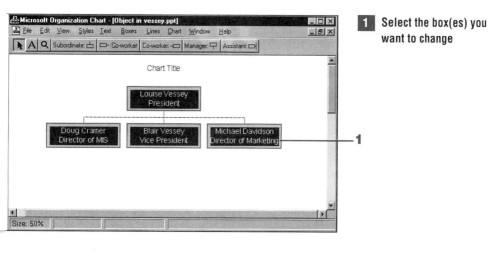

1 Select the box(es) you want to change

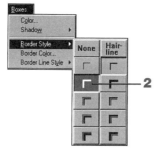

2 Choose Boxes, Border Style, and the style you want

To change the border color or a box

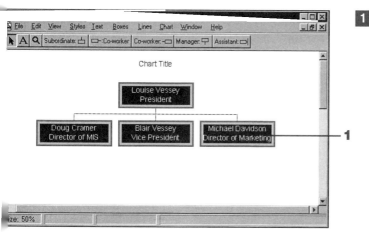

1 Select the box(es) you want to change

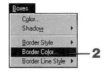

2 Choose Boxes, Border Color

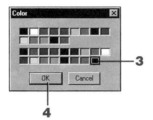

3 Click the new color for the borders

4 Click OK

Note

A colored border on a box should be used for boxes filled with white or another light color. A colored border on boxes with a bright color fill makes the chart hard to read.

To add a shadow to boxes

A shadow behind the boxes makes them appear to be floating above the slide instead of laying right on it.

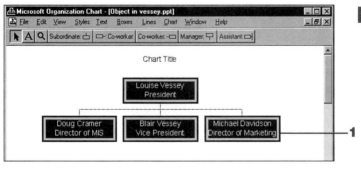

1 Select the box(es) you want to shadow

2 Choose Boxes, Shadow, and the type of shadow you want

To change the background color

If you're using a slide background that is dark, select a matching background color for the organization chart. Remember to check the color of the boxes and text to make sure all the colors you've chosen work for the chart, not against it.

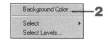

1 Click the right mouse button on the background of the chart

2 Choose Background Color

3 Click the color you want for the background

4 Click OK

Note

The background of the chart stays the color you assign to it regardless of the background color of the slide the chart is on. This can be very effective to emphasize the chart if you choose colors that work well together.

97

Adding Emphasis to Text

You can change the font, style, and size of text in an organization chart, but you can't add effects like underlining or strikethrough.

To change the text attributes

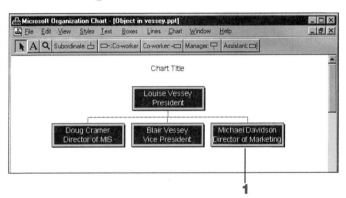

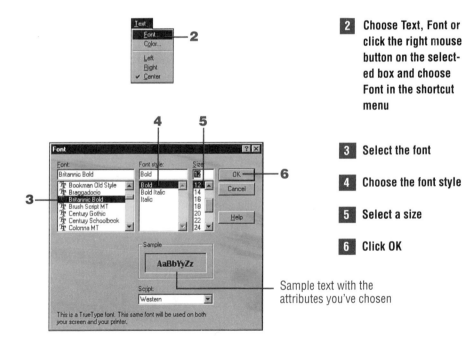

1 Select the box(es) you want to change

Tip You can change attributes for individual pieces of text.

2 Choose Text, Font or click the right mouse button on the selected box and choose Font in the shortcut menu

3 Select the font

6 Click OK

4 Choose the font style

5 Select a size

6 Click OK

Sample text with the attributes you've chosen

To change the color of text

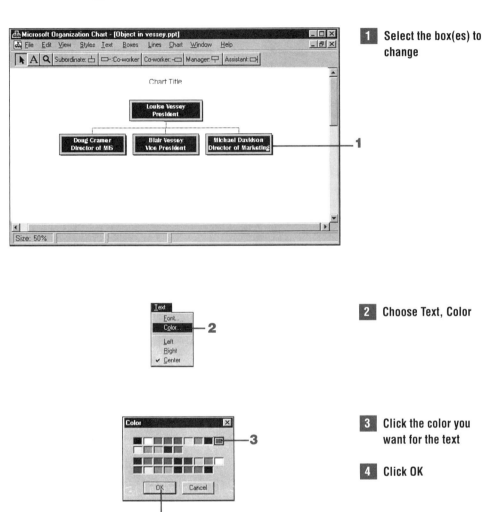

1 Select the box(es) to change

2 Choose Text, Color

3 Click the color you want for the text

4 Click OK

Note

Choose your background color carefully to avoid clashing with your presentation's color scheme.

Changing the Structure on the Organization Chart

You can create five types of boxes on an organization chart for the different positions in your company. You pick the type of box you want to add and then select the box to anchor the new box to.

To add levels

Click these buttons to add the different types of boxes

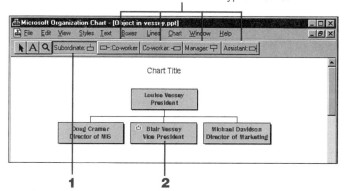

1 Click the type of box you want to add

2 Click the box to connect the new box to

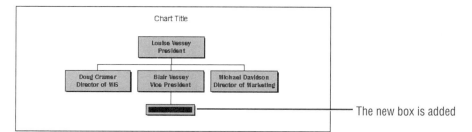

The new box is added

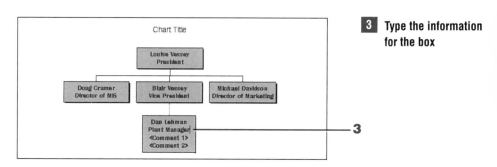

3 Type the information for the box

To change the reporting structure

The superior box changes color when the two boxes are overlapped

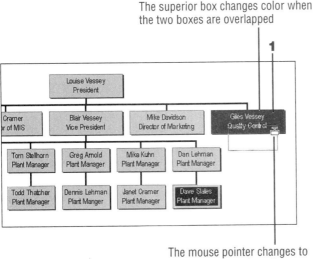

1 Click and drag the box you want to move so it overlaps the box that should be the superior

2 Release the mouse button

The mouse pointer changes to show you're moving a box

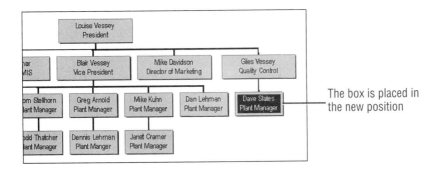

The box is placed in the new position

Note

When you move a box, any boxes that are attached to it also move. To move only the selected box, hold the Control key before you drag the box. The box will be moved to the new location and a blank box will remain in the old location. You can then select the blank box and press Delete to remove it.

To eliminate positions

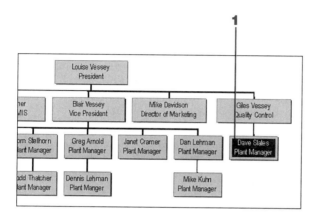

1 Click the box you want to remove

2 Press Delete

Tip If you want to remove several boxes at the same time, use the marquee selector or hold the Shift key while clicking on the boxes you want.

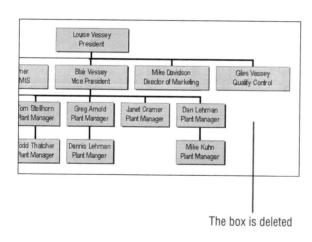

The box is deleted

Changing the Chart's Style

The style of the chart dictates how the boxes are positioned. The default is one top box, with boxes added below the top box in a horizontal row.

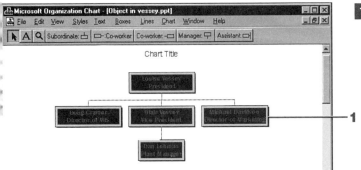

1 Select the boxes in the chart

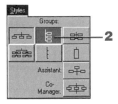

2 Choose Styles, and click the chart style you want

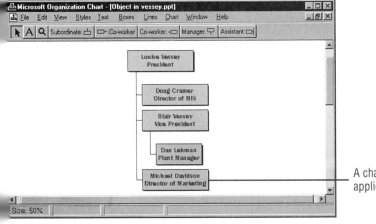

A chart with the new style applied

103

Selecting Parts of an Organization Chart

You can select all the boxes for a certain level, such as managers, while clicking on each and holding the Shift key. An easier way is to use the Select command to select a specific part of the chart.

1 Choose Edit, Select, and the parts you want to select

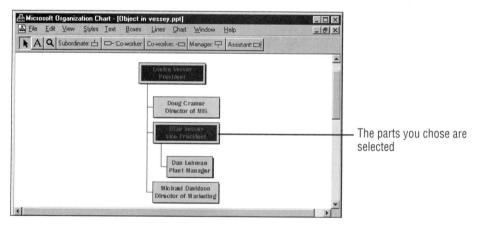

The parts you chose are selected

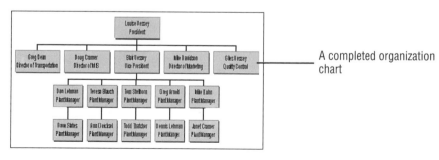

A completed organization chart

When you first start creating a presentation, use the Outline view to organize the information you want to cover. Add the major topics first as the slide headings and then add the points for each slide.

Entering Text

If you use the AutoContent Wizard to set up a presentation, you can replace placeholder text with new text to create an outline. On the other hand, if you start a blank presentation to build an outline, you have to demote text entries yourself to set up the outline.

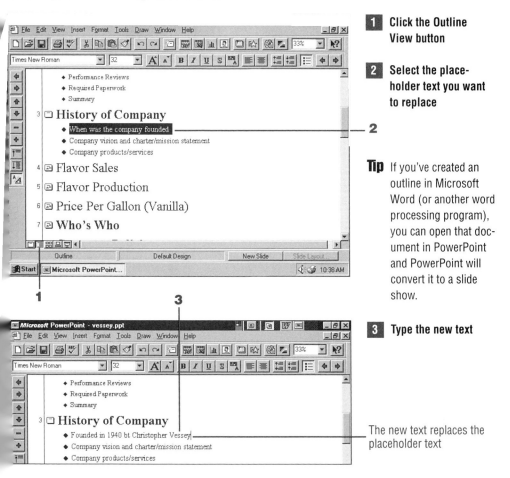

1 Click the Outline View button

2 Select the placeholder text you want to replace

Tip If you've created an outline in Microsoft Word (or another word processing program), you can open that document in PowerPoint and PowerPoint will convert it to a slide show.

3 Type the new text

The new text replaces the placeholder text

Moving Entries

The outline view is best to use when you are organizing your slides. You can move points from one slide to another without having to cut and copy the text.

To move text with the Move button

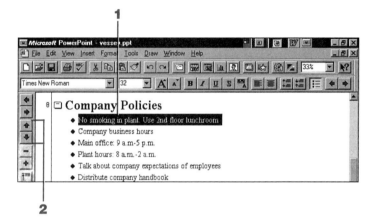

1 Select the text you want to move

2 Click the Move Up or Move Down button once for each line you want to move the selected text over

The text in the new location

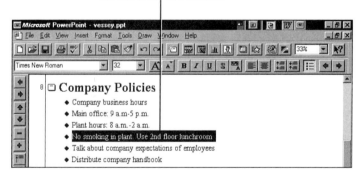

To drag and drop an entry

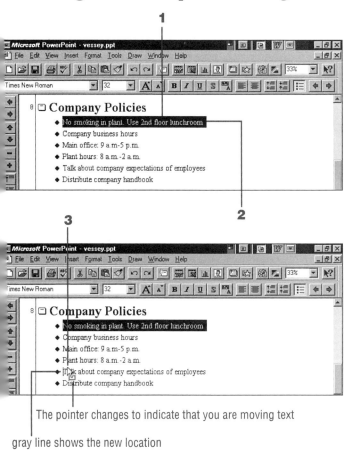

1 Select the entry

2 Click and hold on the entry

The pointer changes to indicate that you are moving text

gray line shows the new location

3 Drag the entry to the new location

4 Release the mouse button

Tip To move an entire slide, click the Slide icon and drag it to the new location. The cursor changes to a four-headed arrow when you position it over the Slide icon. When you click the icon and start dragging, the cursor becomes a two-headed arrow.

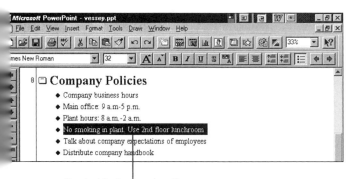

The text in the new location

107

Demoting and Promoting Entries

When you demote an entry, it is indented and the text is made smaller and moved to the right. Promoting the entry enlarges the text and moves it to the left.

To demote entries

1

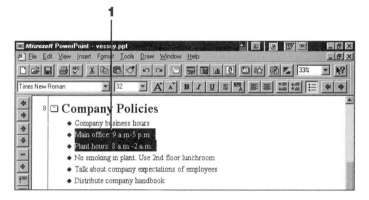

1 Select the text to demote

2 The text is indented and made smaller

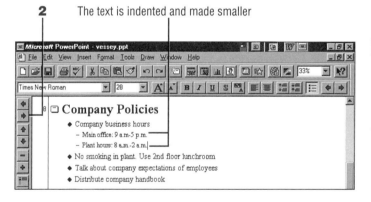

2 Click the Demote (Indent More) button

Tip You can demote an entry up to 5 levels below the slide heading.

To promote entries

2　　**1**

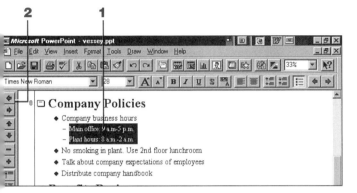

1 Select the text to be promoted

2 Click the Promote (Indent Less) button

The text is moved to the left one level

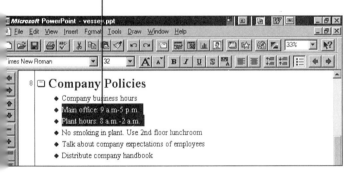

Note

When you promote a text entry, the bullet character changes to match other bullets at that level.

Expanding and Collapsing the Outline

When you can see all the entries under a slide heading, the information for that slide is expanded. When it is collapsed, you can see only the title. When you start a presentation with the AutoContent Wizard, try collapsing the outline text on all the slides so you can concentrate on the slide headings first.

To collapse slide entries

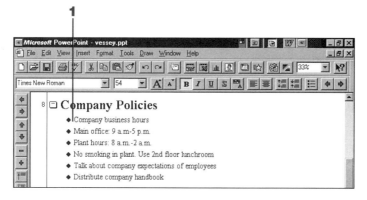

1 Click an insertion point inside the slide text

This gray line indicates a collapsed slide

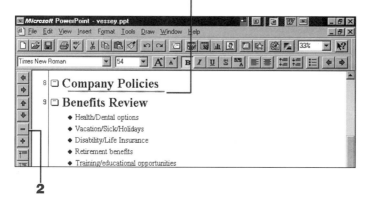

2 Click the Collapse Selection button

110

To expand slide entries

1 Click an insertion point in the slide heading

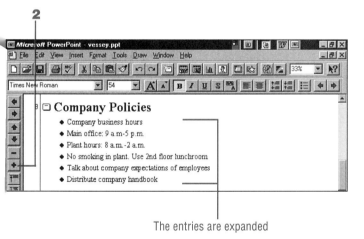

2 Click the Expand Selection button

The entries are expanded

Changing the Formatting of Outline Text

You can apply a style from one section of text to another section. Use the Format Painter to quickly format a single line, but use the Apply Text Style menu command for larger sections of text.

To format a single line

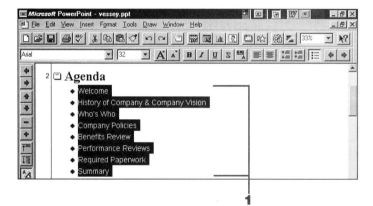

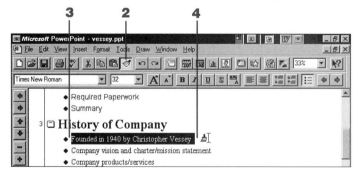

1 Select the text to copy the style from

Tip It's easiest to select the Format Painter right after you finish formatting text in the style you want to apply to all the text. However, you can select any amount of text to copy the style from.

2 Click the Format Painter button

3 Click and hold at the beginning of the text you want to format

4 Drag over the text to select it

5 Release the mouse button

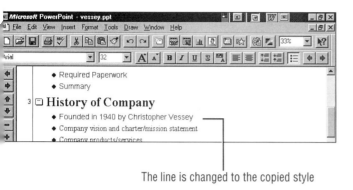

The line is changed to the copied style

To format multiple lines

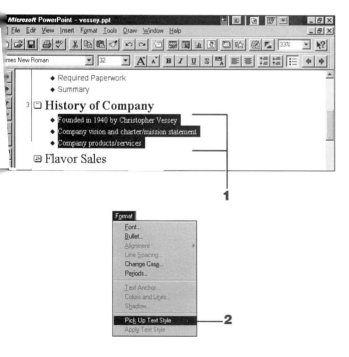

1 Select the text with the style you want to copy

2 Choose Format, Pick Up Text Style

Tip You can also use the Format Painter on large amounts of text. Select the style you want to copy, click the Format Painter, then select all the text to apply the format to.

113

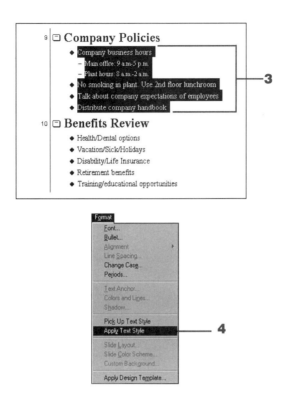

3 Select the text you want to apply the formatting to

4 Choose Format, Apply Text Style

The text is changed to the copied style

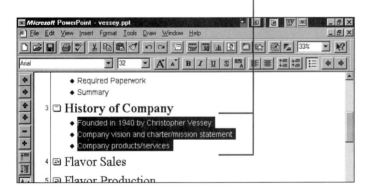

Printing a Presentation

A presentation may be printed to produce copies of the slides, the outline, or notes.

1—

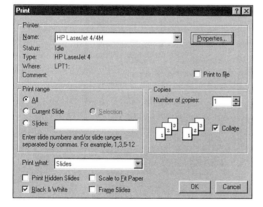

1 Choose File, Print

Tip Click the Print button on the Standard toolbar to print the presentation immediately with the current settings.

2 Change the print settings as necessary (described in the following sections)

3 Click OK to start the print process

Tip Click the Print button in the Standard toolbar to print immediately with the current settings.

To specify the printer settings

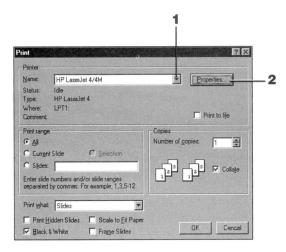

1 In the Print dialog box, select a printer, if necessary

2 Click Properties if you need to change the paper size, orientation, or source, or if you need to change the settings for graphics printing

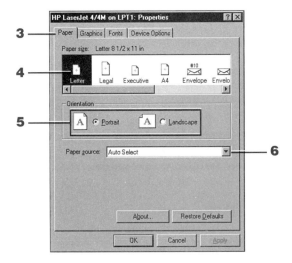

3 Click the Paper tab, if necessary

4 Select a paper size, if necessary

5 Select a paper orientation, if necessary

6 Select a paper source, if necessary

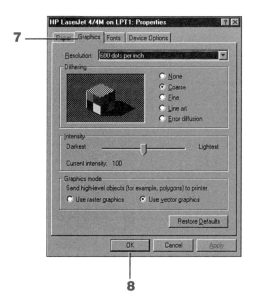

7 Click the Graphics tab if you want to change the settings for producing graphics

8 When you are done changing the printer settings, click OK

Tip Use vector graphics to ensure fastest print speed. If errors appear in the printed graphics, use raster graphics.

Option	Description
Resolution	The number of dots per inch in graphics when they are printed
Dithering	Blends colors to give the appearance of even more colors; also works with white and black to print many shades of gray
Intensity	How dark the graphics will be printed

Note

You can click the Fonts tab and select Print TrueType as Graphics if the presentation contains graphic images.

To set up the print job

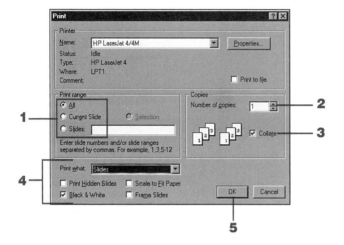

1 In the Print dialog box, select a print range

2 Set the number of copies you want

3 Click this option if you want the copies to be collated as sets (the default setting)

4 Specify which part of the presentation you want to print

5 Click OK

Option	Description
Print What	Select Slides, Handouts (2, 3, or 6 slides per page), Notes Pages, or Outline View
Print Hidden Slides	Prints slides you may have marked as hidden for on on-screen presentaton.
Scale to Fit Paper	Reduces the size of the slide proportionately to fit the size of paper you're using
Frame Slides	Adds a thin line around each slide

Note

The animated printer icon in the status bar displays the number of the slide being processed for printing. Double-click this printer icon to cancel the print job.

118

Previewing the Presentation before Printing

Black and White view provides an on-screen representation of the output of a black-and-white printer. A slide miniature is displayed simultaneously to show the original color view.

1

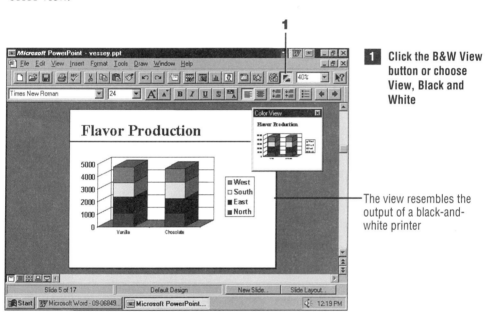

1 Click the B&W View button or choose View, Black and White

The view resembles the output of a black-and-white printer

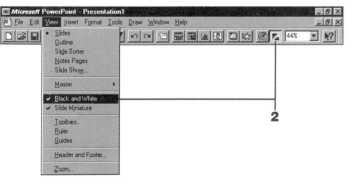

2 When finished viewing, click the B&W View button again or choose View, Black and White again

Tip The Color View window is a slide miniature that shows the original color view.

119

Note

You can display slides faster in Black and White view than in color. Close the small Color View window to reduce even more the amount of Windows resources needed.

Note

Genigraphics will create 35mm slides as well as other color output from your PowerPoint presentation. To pack your presentation and send it to Genigraphics, choose File, Send to Genigraphics. A wizard helps you choose different options for your presentation. Just follow the dialog boxes.

Copying Slides from Another Presentation

You can move or copy slides from another PowerPoint presentation to the one you are currently working on. The information is placed on a new slide in the new presentation and the slide is in the same format as the other slides in the presentation it's copied to, with the same design and color scheme.

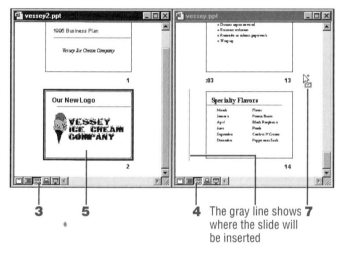

3   **5**

4 The gray line shows **7**
where the slide will
be inserted

The border indicates that   The slide is copied to the presentation
the slide is still selected

1 Open both presentation files

2 Choose Window, Arrange All so you can see both presentations

3 Click the Slide Sorter button in one window

4 Click the Slide Sorter button in the other window

5 Click and hold on the slide you want to move

6 Hold down the Ctrl key

7 Drag to the position in the other presentation where you want to copy the slide

8 Release the mouse button and Ctrl key

121

Creating Builds

All elements of a slide can appear on-screen at once, or you can make elements appear in a special order, one at a time, by building the elements.

To build text only

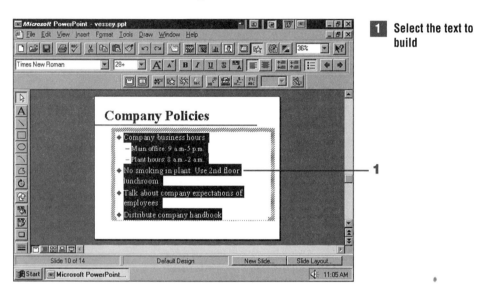

1 Select the text to build

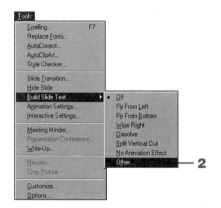

2 Choose Tools, Build Slide Text, and choose Other

Tip You can choose a build effect from the menu, but choosing the Other option lets you simultaneously select other options for the build.

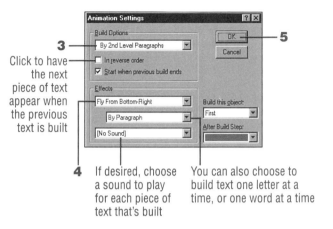

3 Click to have the next piece of text appear when the previous text is built

4 If desired, choose a sound to play for each piece of text that's built

You can also choose to build text one letter at a time, or one word at a time

3 Select the way you want to build text

4 Choose the build effect you want

5 Click OK

To build text and graphics

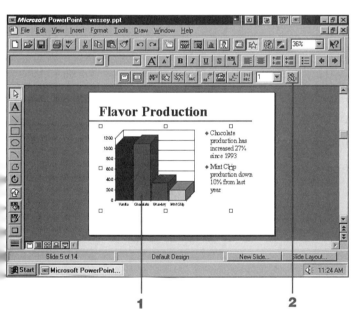

1 Select the graphic

2 Click the Animation Settings button

Tip To display the animation toolbar, choose View, Toolbars, Animation effects, or click the Animation Effects button on the standard toolbar.

Note

If you want to have the text appear first, select the text first and apply the build options. Select the graphic second and apply the build options to it.

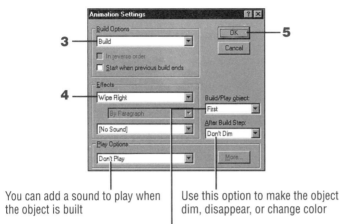 

3 Select Build

4 Choose the desired build effect

5 Click OK

You can add a sound to play when the object is built

Use this option to make the object dim, disappear, or change color

The order the object will appear on the slide— use this object if you have more than one build on the slide

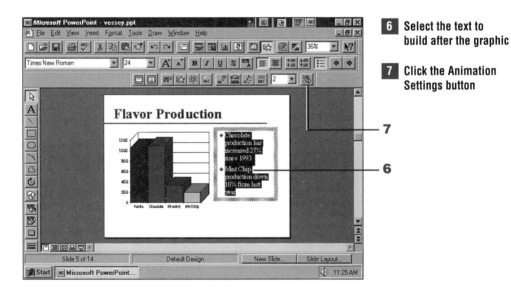

6 Select the text to build after the graphic

7 Click the Animation Settings button

124

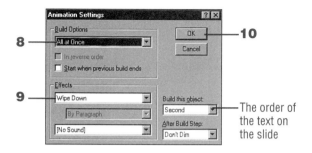

8 — | All at Once

9 — Wipe Down

→ 10

8 Choose the way you want to build the text

9 Select the desired build effect

The order of the text on the slide

10 Click OK

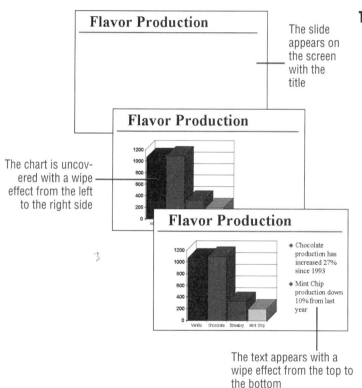

Flavor Production

The slide appears on the screen with the title

Tip Be careful not to use so many special effects that your audience is more interested in watching them than listening to you.

Flavor Production

The chart is uncovered with a wipe effect from the left to the right side

Flavor Production

◆ Chocolate production has increased 27% since 1993

◆ Mint Chip production down 10% from last year

The text appears with a wipe effect from the top to the bottom

Using Transitions

Transitions affect the way a slide appears on-screen after the previous slide ends. You can choose a variety of transition effects, such as having the previous slide "dissolve" into the next slide.

1 Choose Tools, Slide Transition

Tip The transition you set affects the slide that is active.

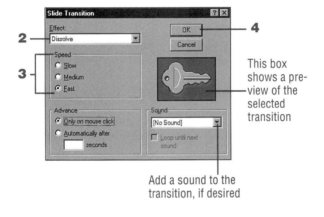

This box shows a preview of the selected transition

Add a sound to the transition, if desired

2 Select the transition effect you want

3 Choose the transition speed

4 Click OK

Running the Slide Show Manually

When you run a slide show manually, you click the mouse button to advance to the next slide. This lets you decide when the next slide should start.

1 Choose View, Slide Show

Tip To view the entire show, move to the first slide of the presentation before selecting Slide Show.

If you want to display only part of the slide show, indicate which slides you want

2 Select Manual Advance and click Show

3 Click the left mouse button to advance from the first slide to the second

4 Continue clicking each time you want to advance to the next slide

Note

You can back up to the preceding slide during a slide show by clicking the right mouse button on the screen. On the pop-up menu, choose Previous.

Setting the Timing to Run a Slide Show Automatically

You can time the slide show to advance the slides automatically as you speak. Before you give the presentation, set the timings while you rehearse your spoken part.

If you want to rehearse only part of the show, indicate which slides you want

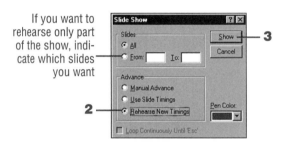

1 Choose View, Slide Show

2 Select Rehearse New Timing

3 Click Show

Note

You can change the timing of the slide show as many times as you need. After you're done timing, you have the option of saving the timing you just completed.

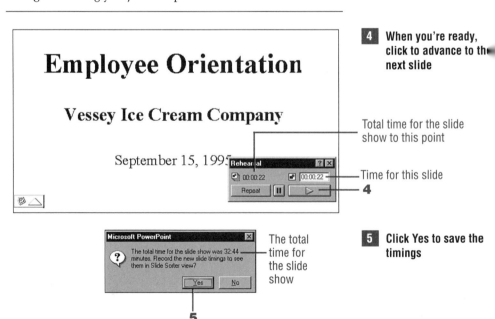

4 When you're ready, click to advance to the next slide

Total time for the slide show to this point

Time for this slide

The total time for the slide show

5 Click Yes to save the timings

Running the Slide Show Continuously

After you set the timings for the slide show, you can choose to have the slide show start from the beginning again when it ends. This could be effective for a presentation set-up for a trade show or other event where people will be passing the computer all the time.

1 Choose View, Slide Show

2 Choose Use Slide Timings

3 Click the Loop Continuously Until 'Esc' option

4 Click Show

Tip To stop the presentation, press Esc.

Note

To prevent viewers from disturbing the show, place the mouse and the keyboard behind the computer while the show is running.

129

Annotating Slides during the Presentation

During the slide show, you may want to mark an item on the slide for emphasis. The Pen tool doesn't mark the slides permanently, and the markings are erased when you advance to the next slide.

To use the pen

1 Click the right mouse button on the slide show screen

2 Choose Pen on the menu

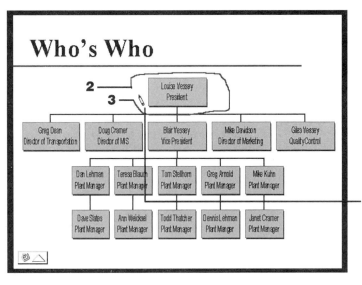

3 Click and hold the mouse button to start drawing

4 Drag the cursor to draw

5 Release the mouse button to stop drawing

The arrow changes to a pencil

To change the pen color

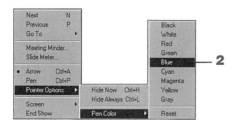

1 Click the right mouse button on the show screen

2 Choose Pointer Options, Pen Color, and the new color you want

Creating and Displaying Hidden Slides

You can choose to move over a hidden slide and not display it, or display it during the presentation. This option is good for a slide you've created with information you may or may not use, such as financial statistics.

To create a hidden slide

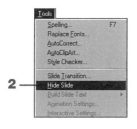

1 Display the slide you want to hide

2 Choose Tools, Hide Slide

Tip To show the hidden slide with no break in the presentation menu, press H.

To display a hidden slide during a presentation

1 Click the right mouse button on the show screen on the slide before the hidden slide

2 Choose Go To, Hidden Slide

131

Ending the Slide Show

When you get to the last slide in the show, the show automatically ends, but you may want to stop the show in the
middle for some reason—for example, if you run out of
time and can't complete the show.

1 Click the right mouse
button on the show
screen

2 Choose End Show
from the menu

Using the Pack & Go Wizard

The Pack & Go Wizard packs your presentation and all the
associated files so you can play the presentation on a computer that doesn't have PowerPoint installed on it. You can
include all the fonts you used as well as any clip art.

To pack a presentation

1 Choose File, Pack
And Go

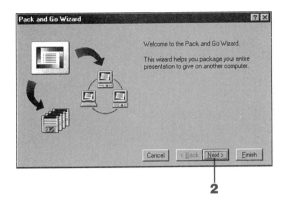

2 Click Next

2

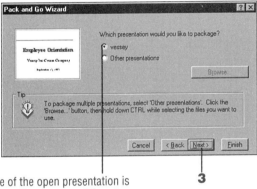

3 Click Next

3

The name of the open presentation is shown here; if you want a different presentation, choose Other Presentation and browse for it

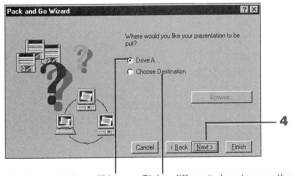

4 Click Next

4

The packed presentation will be saved to a disk in the A drive.

Pick a different place to save the presentation if you want.

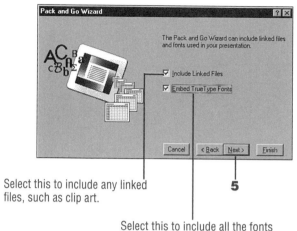

5 Click Next

Select this to include any linked files, such as clip art.

Select this to include all the fonts you used in the presentation.

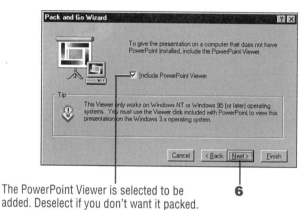

6 Click Next

The PowerPoint Viewer is selected to be added. Deselect if you don't want it packed.

Note

The Viewer that comes with PowerPoint 7 doesn't work on Windows 3.1. If you are showing the presentation on a computer without Windows 95, use the special Windows 3.1 Viewer disk or copy the Windows 3.1 Viewer from the CD to a floppy disk.

Slide Shows: Builds, Transitions, Pack & Go Wizard

7 Click Finish

1 Click the Start button

2 Choose Run

Tip Before you unpack the presentation, you may want to create a special directory on the computer for it.

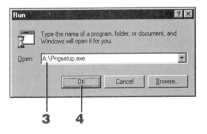

3 Type a:\pngsetup.exe

4 Click OK

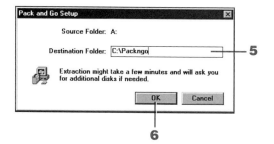

5 Type the name of the directory where the presentation should be unpacked

6 Click OK

7 Click Yes

136

Displaying and Hiding Toolbars

If you don't use a toolbar very often, you may want to hide it so you have more room to work. On the other hand, if you're frequently using one of the non-standard toolbars, consider keeping it displayed all the time.

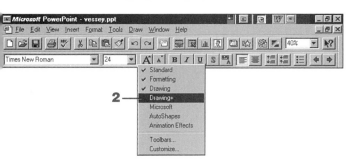

1 Click the right mouse button on a toolbar

2 On the menu, click the toolbar you want to display

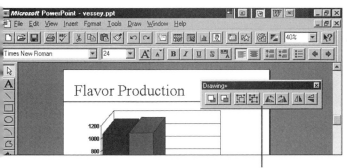

The toolbar appears

Tip To hide a toolbar, repeat the steps.

Note

The toolbar you display may appear anchored to the other toolbars in PowerPoint, or floating on-screen.

Moving Toolbars

You can drag a toolbar around on-screen if it gets in the way while you're working. When you drag the toolbar close to the top, bottom or sides of the screen, it becomes fixed on that side.

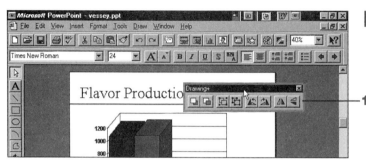

1 Click and hold on the title bar of the toolbar

The gray outline shows the toolbar's new position.

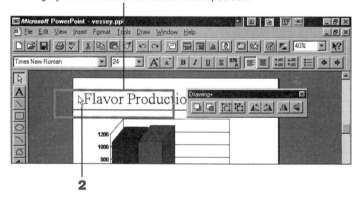

2 Drag the toolbar to the new location

3 Release the mouse button

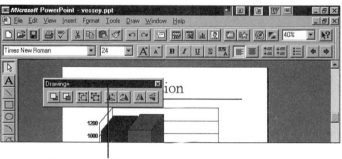

The toolbar in its new location

Tip To move a fixed toolbar, click and drag on a gray area of the toolbar.

Resizing a Floating Toolbar

When you change the size of a floating toolbar, the buttons are rearranged within the new size and shape but don't change shape themselves.

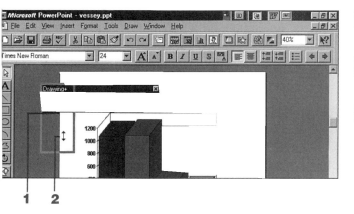

1 Click and hold on the edge of the toolbar

2 Drag the edge to size it

3 Release the mouse button

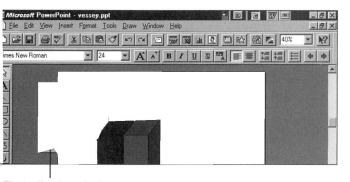

The toolbar is resized

Note

Although you can resize a toolbar both horizontally and vertically, you can't resize it in both directions at once. You must use the sides of the toolbar to resize because you can't drag the corner of the toolbar.

139

Creating Custom Toolbars

You can use the toolbars supplied with PowerPoint or create your own with the tools you use most often.

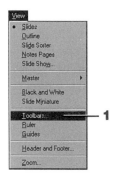

1 Choose View, Toolbars

2 Click New

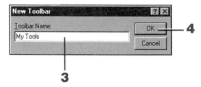

3 Type the name of the new toolbar

4 Click OK

Setting User Options: Toolbars, Rulers, Guides, Buttons

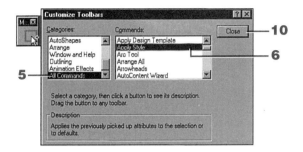

5 Select the category of commands from which you want to use buttons

6 Click and hold on the command

Note

In the All Commands category, only a list is displayed. For all other categories, you see a selection of buttons.

The new toolbar

7 Drag to the new toolbar

8 Release the mouse button

9 Repeat these steps for any other commands you want to add to the toolbar

10 Click Close

141

Changing the Images on the Toolbar Buttons

You can change the picture that appears on each of the toolbar buttons by editing the current picture or creating an entirely new picture.

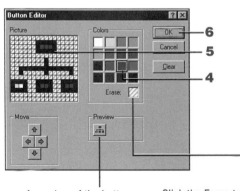

1 Choose Tools, Customize

2 Click the right mouse button on the button you want to change

3 Choose Edit Button Image from the menu

4 Click the color you want to use

5 Click each block in the drawing that you want to change to the new color

6 Click OK

7 Click Close on the Customize Toolbars dialog box

A preview of the button you're creating

Click the Erase tool and click a square to erase the color in that square.

Displaying the Ruler

Use the ruler to draw objects to a specific size or place them on the slide at a specific location. You also use the ruler to add indents and tabs to text.

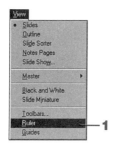

1 Choose View, Ruler

Note

There are actually two rulers—one horizontal and one vertical. However, PowerPoint refers to them as "the ruler." You can't display only one or the other.

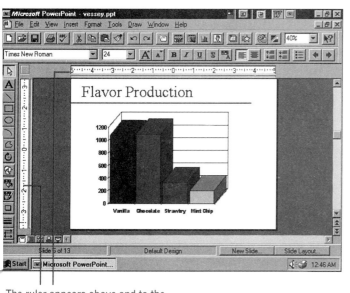

Tip To hide the ruler again, choose View, Ruler.

The ruler appears above and to the left of the slide

Displaying Guides

A horizontal guide and a vertical guide meet in the center
of the slide and appear as dotted lines. Use the guides to
help with placement of objects on the slide.

1 Choose View, Guides

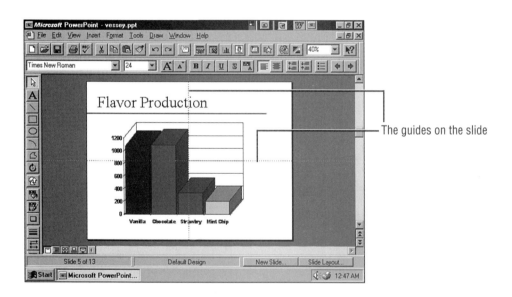

The guides on the slide

Note

You can move a guide to another position on the slide by
clicking and dragging on it. A small marker on the guide
shows you the current position.

Setting Other User Options

The other user options you can choose affect the way PowerPoint does certain tasks, like starting the program or saving files. Other options than those discussed here are available in the same dialog box; this section shows only the options that are particularly useful.

1 Choose Tools, Options

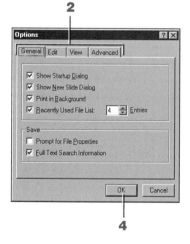

2 Click the tab containing the options you want to change

3 Set the options as desired

4 Click OK when finished making changes

145

Tab	Option	Description
General	Show Startup Dialog	Turn off to start PowerPoint with out the PowerPoint dialog box
General	Recently Used File List	Increase or decrease the number of files shown in the list at the bottom of the File menu
Edit	Drag-and-Drop Text Editing	Turn off if you don't want to use the drag and drop features
Edit	Automatic Word Selection	Turn off if you don't want PowerPoint to automatically select an entire word if you select part of it
View	Status Bar	Turn off to hide the status bar
View	End with Black Slide	Select to finish each slide show with a black screen
Advanced	Maximum Number of Undos	Increase or decrease the number of tasks you can undo

Adding a Table to a Slide

You can add a table to a slide that has a table placeholder, or to one without the placeholder. You can combine a table on a slide with text, if you want, by sizing the table to fit. PowerPoint uses a Microsoft Word table—the same table you use if you are working in Word.

To add a table to a table layout slide

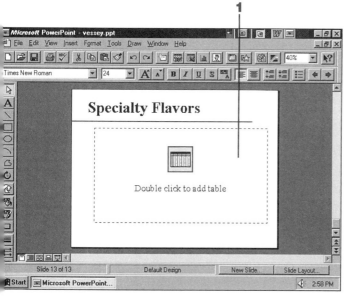

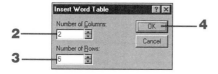

1 Double-click the table placeholder

Tip Double-click in the text box and type the number, or click the up or down arrows to change the setting.

2 Indicate the number of columns

3 Indicate the number of rows

4 Click OK

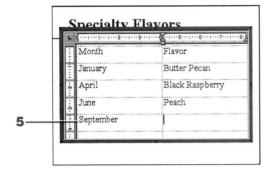

5 Enter the table information (as described
in the section
"Entering Data in the
Table")

6 Click off the table
window

The table on the slide

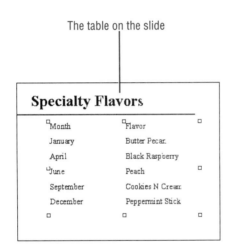

Note

You can also add a table to the slide by choosing Insert,
Microsoft Word Table. In the Insert Word Table dialog box,
enter the number of columns and rows and click OK.

To add a table to a slide without a table placeholder

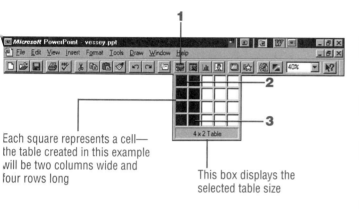

Each square represents a cell—the table created in this example will be two columns wide and four rows long

This box displays the selected table size

1 Click the Insert Microsoft Word Table button

2 Click and hold on the upper left square

3 Drag diagonally to select the size of the table

4 Release the mouse button

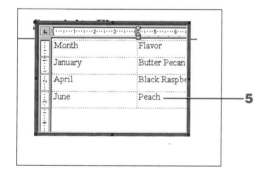

5 Type the table text, as described in the next section

6 Click outside the table window to insert the table into the slide

Entering Data in the Table

Each block in a table where you enter information is called a *cell*. You can enter text in cells and even insert pictures.

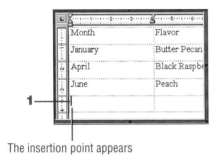

The insertion point appears

1 **Click in the cell where you want to enter data**

Tip Don't press Enter to end a line; the text automatically wraps to the next line. Press Enter only when you want to start a new paragraph within the same cell.

2 **Type the cell text**

3 **Press the Tab key to move to the next column to the right, or Shift+Tab to move to the left**

4 **Continue adding text until the table is complete**

Tip Use the up- and down arrow keys to move to the cell above or below.

Note

If you need to add another row, press the Tab key when you are in the last cell of the table. A new row will be added.

Editing the Data

Edit the information in a table the same way you edit text on a page. You can either replace the entire contents of the cell, or make specific changes.

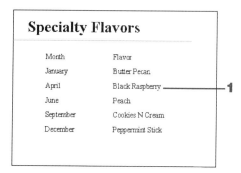

1 Double-click the table in the slide

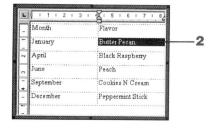

2 Triple-click the cell to highlight all the text in the cell

3 Type the new text

The previous text is replaced by the new text.

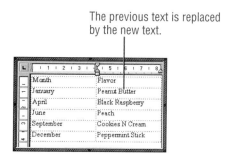

Tip Click once in the cell to add an insertion point. To make slight editorial changes, use the Delete or Backspace key.

Enhancing the Appearance of the Table

PowerPoint relies heavily on visual elements, so you should format tables for the best appearance. You can change the formatting of the text, add borders, and change colors. The easiest way to format a table is to use the AutoFormat command and choose a table style.

To apply Table AutoFormat

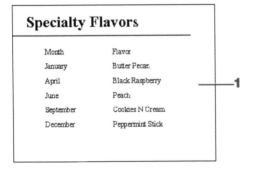

1 Double-click the table in the slide

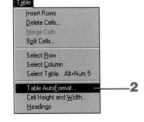

2 Choose Table, Table AutoFormat

Tables: Adding, Entering and Editing Data, Enhancing

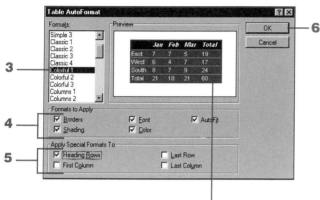

3 Select a format

4 Choose which formats to apply

5 Choose which elements to apply special formats to

6 Click OK

Tip If you don't select the Color option in the AutoFormat dialog box, all the table formats appear in black & white.

A preview of the table changes as you make selections

The table with the AutoFormat applied

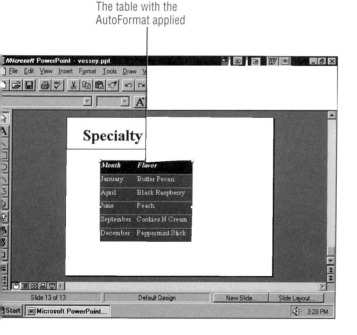

153

To format table text

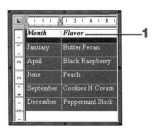

1 In the table window, select the text you want to format

2

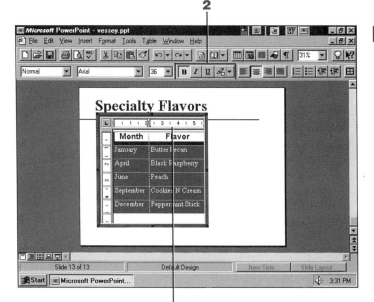

The text changes as you make the selections.

2 Select the new format with the buttons on the Formatting toolba or use the options available on the Formatting menu.

Tip To select several cells, click and hold on the first cell and drag diag onally to the last cell. Release the mouse button.

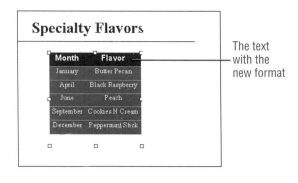

The text with the new format

To change cell height and width

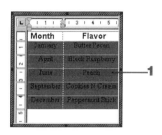

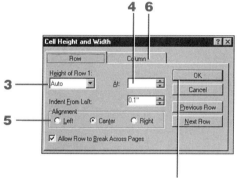

Click OK if you don't want to change the column width.

Enter a new measurement for the space between columns, if desired.

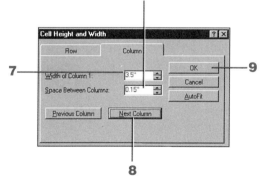

1 Select the cells to change

2 Choose Table, Cell Height and Width

3 Select the row height. (If you don't want to change the height settings, skip to step 6.)

4 If you want a specific height, specify the measurement

5 Choose the alignment for the text in the rows

6 Click the Column tab

Tip Use the Auto setting to have the height set automatically to match the table contents.

7 Enter the width of column 1

8 Click to set the next column and repeat step 7

9 Click OK

155

To add borders to the table

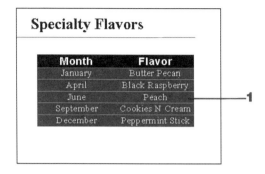

1 Double-click the table in the slide

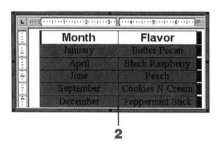

2 Select the cells where you want to add a border

3 Choose Format, Borders and Shading

Click here to add a border only around the perimeter of the table

5

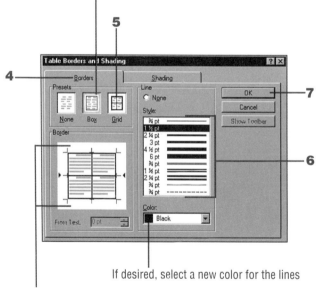

4 If necessary, click the Borders tab

5 Click to add borders around all the cells in the table

6 Select the line style

7 Click OK

If desired, select a new color for the lines

Click any specific lines you want to add or remove

To change the shading
of a table

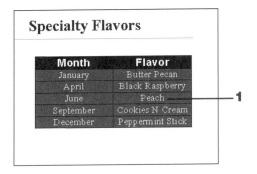

1 Double-click the table in the slide

2 Select the cells you want to change

3 Choose Format, Borders and Shading

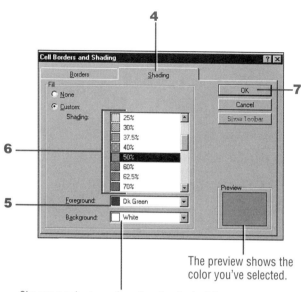

4 Click the Shading tab

5 Choose the color of shading

6 Choose the percentage of shading

7 Click OK

The preview shows the color you've selected.

Choose a color to replace the standard white blocks in a screened pattern, if desired.

Note

Shading is made of small blocks of a dark color, such as black, and a light color, like white. The pattern appears gray when the blocks are black and white. To use the exact color you choose, keep the background color white. For more color options, try changing the background color

The new shading is added to the table.

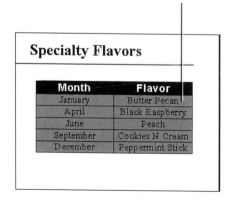

Tip To make the table easy to read, apply one color of shading or fill to the headings and another to the body of the table.

Using Design Templates

The templates in PowerPoint are formatted with a special design background and text and graphics. You don't have to spend hours designing your presentation when you apply a template. You can apply the template before you add your text, or while you are working on the presentation.

To create a new presentation with a template

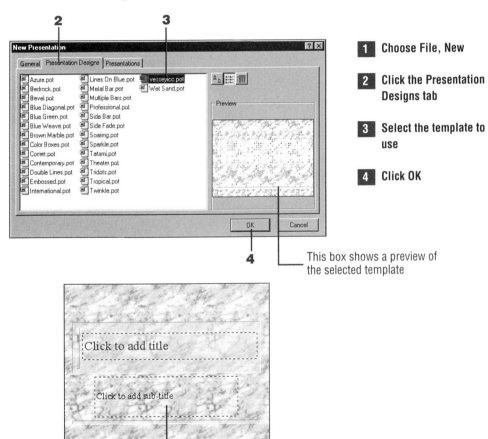

1 Choose File, New

2 Click the Presentation Designs tab

3 Select the template to use

4 Click OK

This box shows a preview of the selected template

The first slide with the selected design template

To apply a new design template

1 Choose Format, Apply Design Template

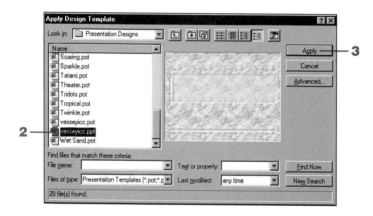

2 Select the template to apply

3 Click Apply

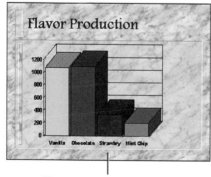

The template is applied to all slides in the presentation.

Tip Not all the templates will look terrific on every one of the slides. Review each slide carefully to make sure the template and the objects on the slides don't clash.

Creating a Design Template

You can create a design template from scratch, but it's easiest to modify an existing template. After you modify the template, save it so that you can use it over and over again.

To open an existing template

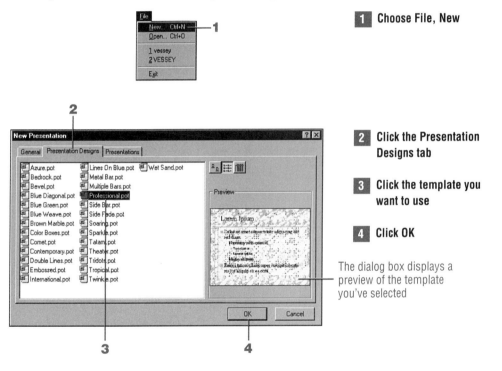

1 Choose File, New

2 Click the Presentation Designs tab

3 Click the template you want to use

4 Click OK

The dialog box displays a preview of the template you've selected

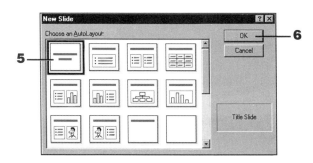

5 Select the first slide
layout

6 Click OK

The first slide using the template
you selected

Note

Colorful slides are a good way to keep your audience interested, but be careful not to go overboard on the amount of color.
If you're using a lot of graphs and tables with color, use a
muted background. For mostly plain text, you can add more
color on the background.

To change the color scheme

1 Choose Format, Slide Color Scheme

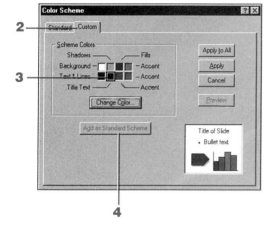

2 Click the Custom tab

3 Click the color you want to change

4 Click Change Color

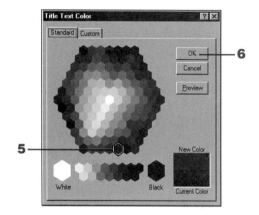

5 Click a new color to replace the one you selected

6 Click OK

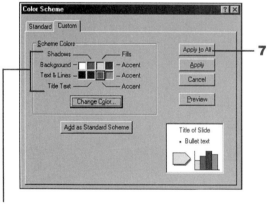

Repeat the steps for each color you want to change.

7 Click Apply to All

Tip Click the Apply button if you want to make the changes only on the current slide.

To change the slide master

1 Choose View, Master, Slide Master

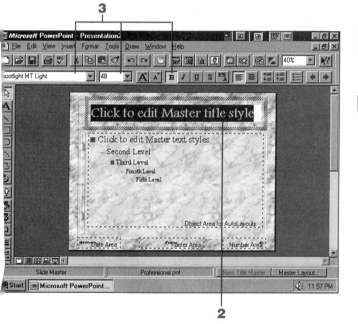

2 Select the placeholder text for the item you want to change

3 Choose the new formatting for the text with the buttons on the Formatting toolbar or the options available on the Format menu.

165

To save the new slide master

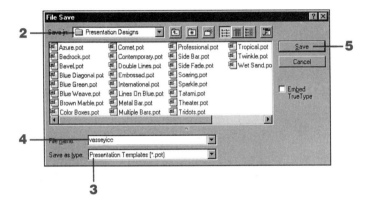

1 Choose File, Save As

2 Select the drive and folder where you want to save the file

3 Select the file type: Presentation Templates (*.pot)

4 Type the name of the file

5 Click OK

Using ClipArt Images in Slides

There are two slide layouts that contain a placeholder for clip art. Each of these also contains a placeholder for text. The Microsoft ClipArt Gallery contains many types of clip art, such as art for business or sports clip art.

Adding clip art to a ClipArt Slide

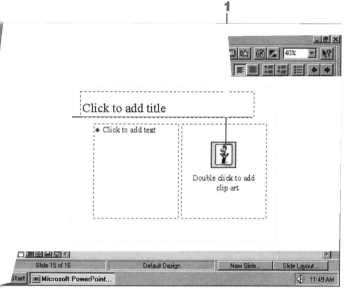

1 Double-click on the clip art placeholder

Tip The first time you use ClipArt, you may get a message asking if you want to add any installed images to the ClipArt Gallery. You can then select the sets of clip art you want to add. This may take a few minutes.

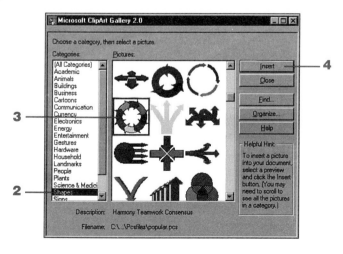

2 Select the desired category of clip art

3 Click the clip art you want

4 Click Insert

Tip A description of each piece of clip art appears at the bottom of the dialog box.

167

Adding clip art to any slide

You don't need a clip art slide layout to add clip art. You can add clip art to any slide in your presentation.

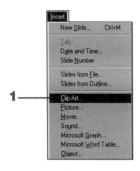

1 Choose Insert, Clip Art

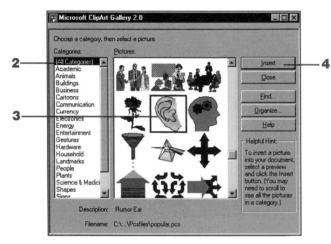

2 Choose the category of clip art

3 Select the clip art you want

4 Click Insert

Tip The clip art you choose won't be as small as in the dialog box after it's placed on the slide. It will be much bigger and you'll see more detail.

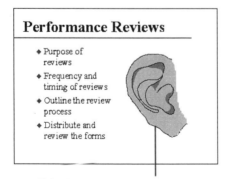

This clip art was moved and resized on this slide.

Replacing a clip art image

Instead of deleting a piece of clip art because you don't like it, just replace it. The new clip art will be added to the same spot.

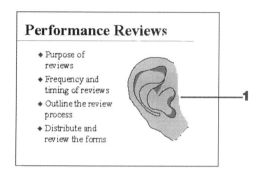

1 Double-click on the current clip art

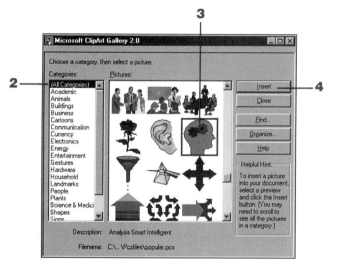

2 Select the clip art category

3 Click on the clip art you want to use

4 Click Insert

The old clip art is replaced with the new

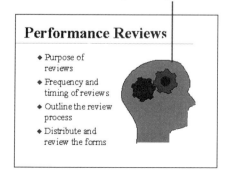

169

Using AutoClipArt

The AutoClipArt feature scans your presentation and matches clip art to key words it finds. You can choose to insert each piece of suggested clip art or to ignore it.

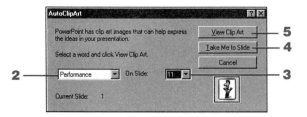

1 Choose Tools, AutoClipArt

2 Select a key word in the list

3 Select the slide number the key word appears on

Note

The Take Me to Slide option is grayed; you can't use it if the slide with the keyword is the current slide or if there is only one slide in the presentation with keywords.

4 Click Take Me to Slide

5 Click View Clip Art

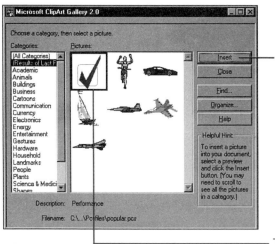

The suggested clip art is selected

6 Select the image you want in the suggested set

7 Click Insert to add the clip art to the slide

8 Repeat the steps as desired for additional key words and clip art

9 When you're done adding clip art, click Cancel

The clip art is added to the slide

10 To move or resize the clip art, select it, and then drag the image to move it or drag a handle to resize it

Adding an image to the ClipArt Gallery

You can add images—including bitmaps and Paint files—
to the ClipArt Gallery so you can access them easily every
time you need them.

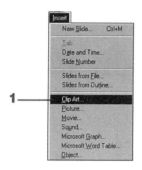

1 Choose Insert, ClipArt

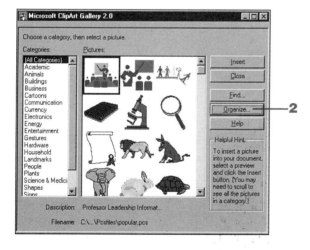

2 Click Organize

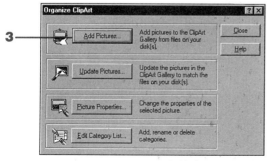

3 Click Add Pictures

4 Select the drive and folder containing the clip art you want to add

5 Click the file name of the clip art

6 Click Open

7 Type a name for the clip art

8 Click the boxes of the categories in which you want the clip art displayed (optional)

9 Click OK

Click to add a new category to the list

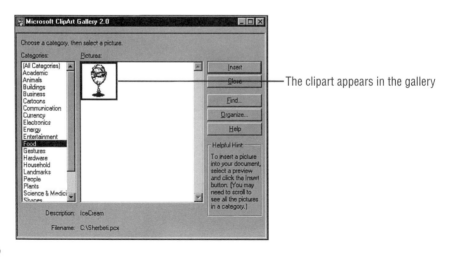

The clipart appears in the gallery

Recoloring clip art

You can change the original colors of clip art from the
gallery to suit your presentation.

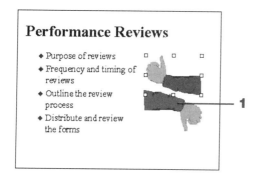

1 Click once on the clip
art to select it

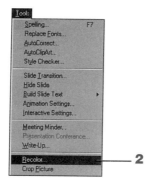

2 Choose Tools,
Recolor

These boxes show the original colors that you're changing;
the number of boxes and matching palettes depends on
the number of colors in the image

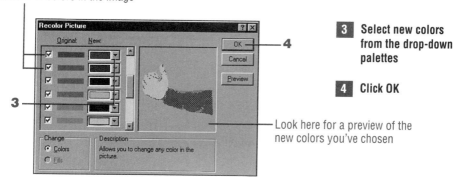

3 Select new colors
from the drop-down
palettes

4 Click OK

Look here for a preview of the
new colors you've chosen

Cropping clip art images

You crop clip art to remove a part of the image, without changing the overall image size. Crop out the part you don't want.

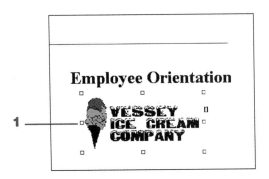

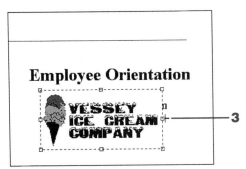

1 Click the clip art once to select it

2 Choose Tools, Crop Picture

3 Click on a handle

4 Hold down the left mouse button

5 Drag the handle toward the center of the clip art

6 Release the mouse button

Note

You can get back the area of clip art you cropped. With the cropping tool, click on the same handle you used before and drag the handle in the opposite direction until the part you want back is exposed.

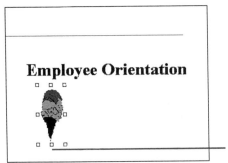

The text was cropped off this piece of clip art

Adding a Movie to a Slide

A movie in AVI format can be inserted into a slide. You'll be able to play the movie during the presentation.

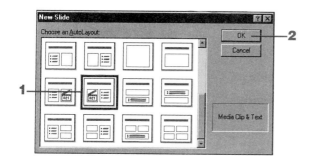

1 Insert a new slide, selecting a Media Clip and Text slide format

2 Click OK

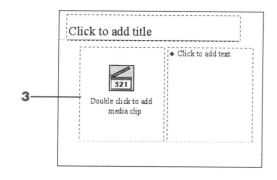

3 Double-click the media clip placeholder

4 Choose Insert Clip, Video for Windows

175

Note

The advantage of using the Insert Clip, Video for Windows command is that it automatically searches only for files that fit its description.

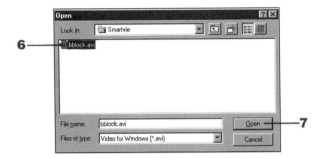

5 Select the drive and folder containing the movie clip

6 Click on the file name

7 Click Open

Click the Play button to play the clip

The clip is inserted in the slide.

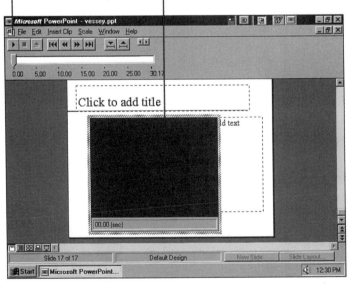

Inserting Sound Files or Music in a Slide

You can add a sound clip to a slide, either in WAV or MIDI format, and you can also add a portion of an audio CD if your CD-ROM drive plays audio CDs.

To insert a sound clip (WAV format)

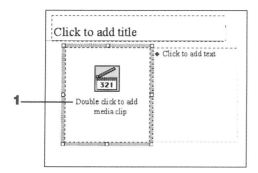

1 Double-click the media clip placeholder

2 Choose Insert Clip, Sound

Note

You can resize the sound clip box on a slide by dragging the handles. If you have a lot of text on the same slide, you can make the clip small so that it's hardly noticeable.

3 Select the drive and folder containing the sound clip

4 Click the file name

5 Click Open

Click the Play button to play the clip

The sound clip

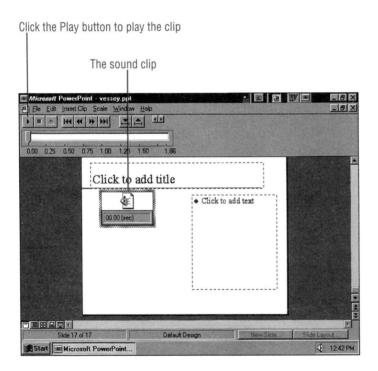

To insert a music clip (MIDI format)

1 Choose Insert Clip, MIDI Sequencer

2

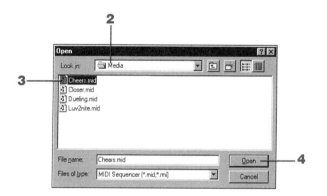

2 Select the drive and folder containing the music clip

3 Click on the file name

4 Click Open

lick to stop playing the clip

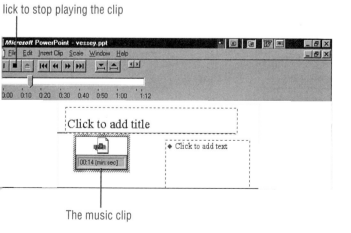

The music clip

To add an audio CD clip

1 Choose Insert Clip, CD Audio

Tip Before you add the CD clip, put the CD in the drive.

Click to play the CD

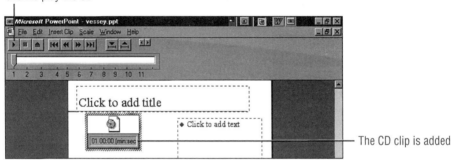

The CD clip is added

Using the Media Player

The Media Player controls how sound and music clips are played. You can use it to play parts of a clip, such as one track of a CD, to repeat a selection in a loop, or to control the volume of the clip.

To select part of a clip

1 Choose Edit, Selection

180

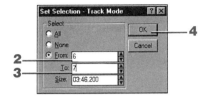

2 Set the starting point of the selection

3 Set the ending point of the selection

4 Click OK

Click to play the selection

Click to stop playing

Tip To select one track from an audio CD, enter the track number you want to play in the From text box and enter the track number you want to stop at in the To text box. You don't need to put in the specific times.

The selected range is shown in black; only that area will be played

To repeat the selection continuously

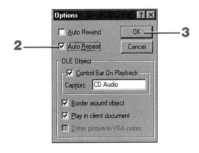

1 Choose Edit, Options

2 Click the Auto Repeat option

3 Click OK

To adjust the volume of the media clip

1 Choose Edit, Volume Control

Click and drag this button to
control the master volume

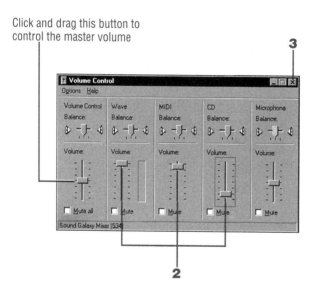

2 Click and drag the appropriate button to adjust the clip

3 Click the close button to close the volume control window

Drawing Objects

PowerPoint contains several tools for drawing objects as you would in a drawing program. If you want any objects to appear on all the slides in your presentation, create the objects on the master slide.

To draw a specific shape

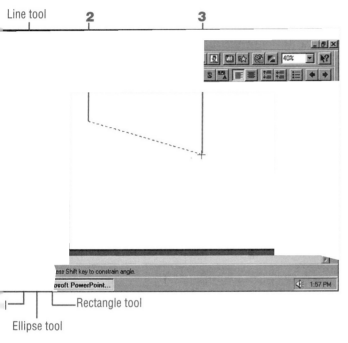

Line tool
2   **3**

Rectangle tool

Ellipse tool

1 Click the tool for the shape you want (see the table for details)

2 Click where you want to start drawing

3 Drag the mouse horizontally, vertically, or diagonally until the object is the desired shape and size

4 Release the mouse button

Tool	Description
Line	Draws a straight line; press Shift while dragging to keep the line at 45° angles
Rectangle	Draws a rectangle; press Shift while dragging to create a square
Ellipse	Draws an ellipse; press Shift while dragging to create a circle
Arc	Draws an arc; after clicking the endpoint, drag the arc until the shape is correct

183

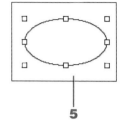

5 To resize or reshape the object, click the object and drag the handles

Tip Use the corner handles to size horizontally and vertically in proportion; use the side handles to widen or narrow; use the top or bottom handles to heighten or shorten.

To create a freeform drawing

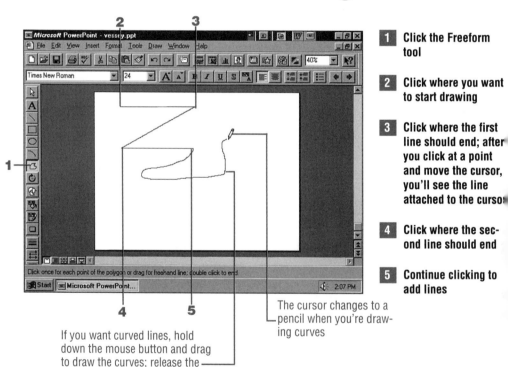

1 Click the Freeform tool

2 Click where you want to start drawing

3 Click where the first line should end; after you click at a point and move the cursor, you'll see the line attached to the cursor

4 Click where the second line should end

5 Continue clicking to add lines

The cursor changes to a pencil when you're drawing curves

If you want curved lines, hold down the mouse button and drag to draw the curves; release the mouse button to stop drawing

Manipulating Groups of Objects

Grouped objects essentially become one object while retaining their original formatting, such as fill and line color and width. You can move several objects together by grouping them.

To group objects

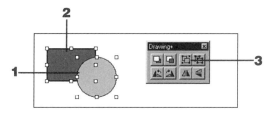

Handles appear around both objects to show they're grouped.

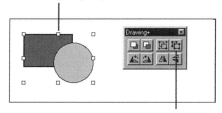

Click the Ungroup button if you want to ungroup the objects.

To stack objects

Objects appear on the slide in the order they are created. If you move several objects on top of each other, you may want to change the order of them. Use the Bring Forward and Send Backward buttons to do that.

Bring Forward button ———— Send Backward button

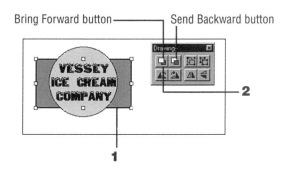

1 Click the first object

2 Hold down the Shift key, and then click the next object. Hold the Shift key until you are done selecting

3 When you are done selecting, click the Group button on the Drawing+ toolbar

Tip To show the Drawing+ toolbar, right-click on an active toolbar and choose Drawing+ from the shortcut menu.

1 Select the object

2 Click the Bring Forward/Send Backward button once for each level you want to move forward/backward in the stack

185

Rotating and Flipping Objects

All objects can be rotated in either 90-degree increments or a full 360 degrees. Objects can also be flipped horizontally and vertically, with the exception of text that cannot be flipped horizontally.

To rotate 90° to the right or left

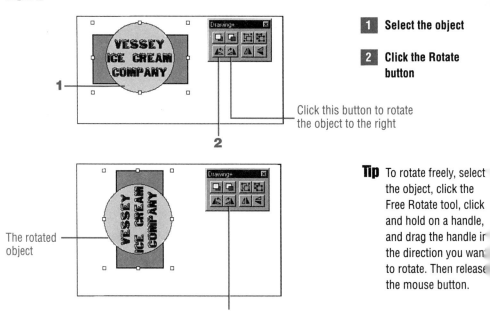

1 Select the object

2 Click the Rotate button

Click this button to rotate the object to the right

The rotated object

Click to return the object to its previous position.

Tip To rotate freely, select the object, click the Free Rotate tool, click and hold on a handle, and drag the handle in the direction you want to rotate. Then release the mouse button.

To flip an object

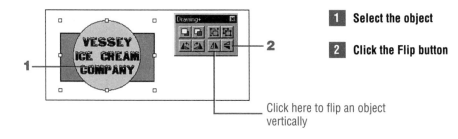

1 Select the object

2 Click the Flip button

Click here to flip an object vertically

Adding Fills and Shadows

The fill of an object is the color that appears inside it. You can choose any color from the palette for the fill, as well as use the special pattern, texture, and shading fills that can be applied to the background. A shadow behind an object makes the object appear to be floating in front of the slide.

To add a fill

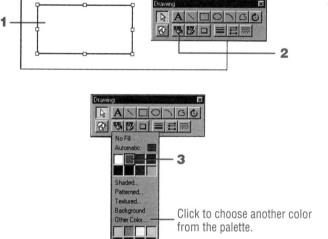

1 Select the object

2 Click the Fill button

3 Click the fill you want to add

Click to choose another color from the palette.

To add a shadow

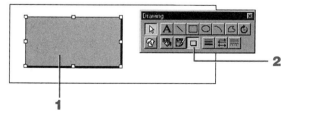

1 Select the object

2 Click the Shadow button

187

To use a transparent fill

A semi-transparent fill in an object lets the object behind it show through a bit. This option is available for all solid-color fills but not the special fills, such as patterns or textures.

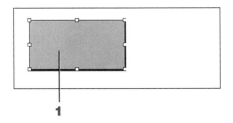

1 Select the object

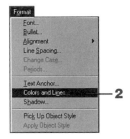

2 Choose Format, Colors and Lines

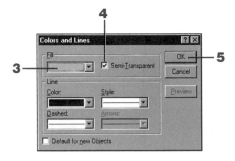

3 Select the color for the object's fill

4 Choose the Semi-transparent option

5 Click OK

Animating Objects

Every object you create can be animated so it appears on
the screen during the slide show in a special way. You
decide the order the objects appear on-screen as well.

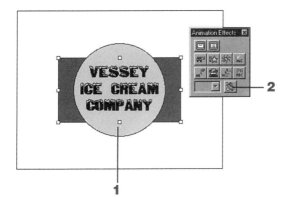

1 Select the object (to
animate several
objects together,
group them first)

2 Click the Animation
Settings button

Tip To display the
Animation Effects
toolbar, click the
Animation Effects
button on the Standard
toolbar.

Note

If you're planning to animate several objects on the same
slide, decide the order in which they should appear. Then add
the animation effects in that order.

Select this if you want to build the
next object when the first object is
finished—so you don't have to click
the mouse.

This should be the order you're
creating the animations in.

3 Choose Build

4 Select the animation
effect for the object

5 Click OK

6 Select the next object
to animate

7 Repeat steps 1-6 until
the animations are
complete

189

Index

Symbols

3-D graphs, 27
3-D View command (Format menu), 29

A

Advanced tab, 146
aligning text
    line spacing, 57
    paragraphs, 56
Alignment command
    (Format menu), 56
animating text, 77-78
Animation toolbar,
    displaying, 123
annotating slides during presentations, 130
Apply Design Template command (Fiormat menu), 160
Apply Text Styles
    command (Format menu), 114
audio
    Media Player
        selecting clips, 180-181
        volume, 182
    MIDI format, 179-180
    WAV format, 177-178
    in slides, 177-180
AutoClipArt, 170
AutoClipArt command
    (Tools menu), 170
AutoContent Wizard, 5-15
AutoCorrect, 48
    adding words to, 49
    deleting words, 49
AutoCorrect command
    (Tools menu), 48
AutoFormat feature, formatting tables, 152-153

B

background
    muted backgrounds, 162
    organization charts, 97
    slides
        adding clip art, 72
        adding patterns, 70
        adding shade, 68-69
        adding texture, 71
Background command
    (Chart menu), 97

Border Style command
    (Boxes menu), 95
borders
    adding to tables, 156
    organization charts, 95-96
Borders and Shading
    command (Format menu), 156
Boxes menu commands, 94-97
Build Slide Text command
    (Tools menu), 122
builds
    graphics, 123-125
    text, 122-125
Bullet command
    (Format menu), 59
bullets, paragraphs, 59-60
buttons, customizing, 142

C

canceling print job, 118
cells,
    datasheets
        editing information, 24
        entering information, 21
    tables
        borders, 156
        editing data in, 151
        entering data into, 150
        formatting, 152-155
        shading, 157-158
Chart menu, 97
charts, see organization charts
Clear command
    (Edit menu), 37
clip art
    adding to handouts, 87
    adding to notes, 87
    coloring, 173
    Microsoft ClipArt Gallery, 167-169
        adding images, 171-172
        coloring, 173
    moving, 170
    placeholders, 167
    replacing, 169
    resizing, 170
    slides, 167-168, 170
        AutoClipArt, 170
        cropping, 174

    replacing, 169
    as slide background, 72
    see also graphics, 87
Clip Art command
    (Insert menu), 86
Clipboard (Windows), 43
collapsing text in
    placeholders, 110
color
    graphs, 30-31
    organization charts, 94
    pen, 131
    presentations, changing, 76
    slides, 162-164
    text, organization charts, 99
Color command
    Boxes menu, 94
    Text menu, 99
Color Scheme
    dialog box, 31
coloring clip art, 173
columns
    changing space between, 28
    graphs, 32
    tables, width, 155
commands, see individual listings
Copy command
    (Edit menu, 44
copying text, 44
Crop Picture command
    (Tools menu), 174
cropping clipart, 174
Custom Background
    command (Format menu), 68-72
Custom Background
    dialog box, 70-72
Custom toolbars, creating, 140-141
Customize command
    (Tools menu), 142
customizing
    organization charts
        background, 97
        borders, 95-96
        color, 94
        line widths, 93
        shadows, 96-97

191

toolbar buttons, 142
Cut command
  (Edit menu), 43
cutting text, 43

D

Data menu commands,
  Exclude Row/Column, 22
Datasheet window, 21, 24
datasheets, entering
  information into cells, 21
Date and Time command
  (Insert menu), 85
dates
  adding to handouts, 85
  adding to notes, 85
  adding to presen-
    tations, 75
Delete Slide command (Edit
  menu), 11
deleting
  AutoCorrect entries, 49
  graphs, 37
  slides, 11
  text characters, 40
demoting text in
  placeholders, 108
deselecting text, 8
Design template, creating
  presentations, 159
  applying Design Template,
    160
  creating Design Template,
    161-162
dictionary (spell checker),
  adding names, 47
displaying
  Animation toolbar, 123
  guides, 144
  ruler, 143
  Shortcut menu, 44
  slides, hidden slides, 131
  toolbars, 137
dithering, defined, 117
drag and dropping text, 46,
  107
dragging toolbars, 138-139
drawing
  shapes, 183
  freeforms, 184

E

Edit menu commands, see
  individual commands
Edit tab, 146
editing
  data entries in tables, 151
  organization charts,
    91-92
  paragraphs, bullets, 59-60
  slide master, 65-66
    deleting characters, 40
    replacing existing
      text, 41
effects, animation of text,
  77-78
ending slide shows, 132
Exit command (File menu),
  18, 90
exiting presentations, 18
expanding text in
  placeholders, 111

F

File menu commands, see
  individual commands
files
  naming, 14
  opening, 15
  saving, 14
fills
  adding, 187
  transparent, 188
Find command
  (Edit menu), 61
finding text, 61
floating toolbars,
  sizing, 139
Font command
  Format menu, 33, 55
  Text menu, 98
fonts
  attributes, applying
    multiple, 55
  changing, 52
  formatting in graphs, 33
  organization charts, 98
  sizing, 53
  styles, applying, 54
footers
  adding to handouts, 84
  adding to notes, 84
  creating, 74
  formatting text in, 86

Format menu commands,
  see individual commands
Format Painter feature, 112
formats, slides, 73
formatting
  graphs, 26
    color scheme, 30-31
    columns, 28
    depths, 27
    numbers, 34
    rotating, 29
    see also graphs, 37
  tables
    AutoFormat, 152-153
    borders, 156
    cells, 155
    shading, 157-158
    text, 154
  text
    graphs, 33
    in headers/footers, 86
    in placeholders,
      112-114

G

Genigraphics, 120
Genral tab, 146
graphics
  adding to handouts, 87
  adding to notes, 87
  dithering, 117
  Genigraphics, 120
  intensity, 117
  raster, 117
  resolution, 117
  slide builds, 123-125
  vector, 117
  see also clip art, 87
graphs
  adding to slides, 19-20
  color scheme, 31
  columns, 32
  deleting, 37
  editing information
    in, 24
  entering information, 21
  formatting, 26
    color scheme, 30
    columns, 28
    depth, 27
    numbers, 34
    rotating, 29
  legends, adding/
    removing, 36

resizing, 35
restoring, 37
rows, 32
saving as standard, 31
spreadsheet tables, 22-23
subtypes, 26
choosing, 26
text
font, 33
formatting, 33
types of, changing, 25
guides
displaying, 144
moving, 144
Guides command
(View menu), 144

H

handouts
creating, 83
dates, adding, 85
headers/footers, adding
to, 84
printing, 88
Header and Footer
command (View
menu), 74
headers
adding to handouts, 84
adding to notes, 84
creating, 74
formatting text in, 86
Height and Width
command (Table
menu), 155
Help dialog box, 3
Hide Slide command (Tools
menu), 131
hiding
ruler, 143
tips, 3
toolbars, 137

I-K

indenting text, 108-109
Insert menu commands,
10, 85-86
inserting
footers into slides, 74
graphs into slides, 19-20
headers into slides, 74
slides into presen-
tations, 10

tables into slides, 147-149
text into existing text, 42
intensity, defined, 117

L

layout
notes, changing, 80
slides, changing, 67
legends (graphs)
adding/removing, 36
restoring, 36
Line Spacing command
(Format menu), 57
lines
organization charts, changing widths, 93
spacing, 57

M

Master command
(View menu), 65
Media Player
selecting clips, 180-181
volume, 182
menus (shortcut),
displaying, 44
Microsoft ClipArt Gallery,
167-169
adding images, 171-172
coloring, 173
Microsoft Office,
shortcut bar, 3
MIDI format, 179-180
movies, slides, 175-176
moving
boxes in organization
charts, 101-102
guides, 144
slides, 9, 13
text in placeholders, 106
toolbars, 138
music
in slides, 179-180
Media Player
selecting clips, 180-181
volume, 182
music clips (MIDI format),
179-180

N

naming files, 14
navigating presentations, 9

New command
(File menu), 17, 159
New Slide command (Insert
menu), 10
notes
creating, 79
dates, adding, 85
headers/footers,
adding to, 84
layout, 80
master pages,
changing, 82
pages, sizing, 79
printing, 88
sizing notes box, 81
Notes Pages command (View
menu), 79
Number command
(Format menu), 34
numbers (graphs),
formatting, 34

O

objects
animating, 189
drawing, 183
flipping, 186
grouping, 185
manipulating groups, 185
rotating, 186
stacking, 185
Open command
(File menu), 15
opening
files, 15
presentations, 15
templates, existing,
161-162
options, setting, 145
Options command
(Tools menu), 145
organization charts
creating, 89-90
customizing
background, 97
borders, 95-96
color, 94
line width, 93
shadows, 96-97
editing, 91-92
moving boxes, 101-102
selecting parts of, 104

structure
adding levels, 100
reporting structure,
101-102
styles, 103
text
color, 99
fonts, 98
orientation, slides, 73
Outline View, 106
outlines, text
collapsing, 110
demoting, 108
drag and drop, 107
entering, 105
expanding, 111
formatting, 112-114
moving, 106
promoting, 109
Overstrike mode, 41

P

Pack and Go command (File
menu), 132
Pack and Go Wizard,
132-136
packing presentations,
132-136
paragraphs
alignment, 56
bullets, 59-60
spacing, 58
Paste command
(Edit menu), 45
pasting text, 45
patterns (slides), adding, 70
Pen feature, 130-131
pictures, *see* graphics, 87
placeholders
clipart, 167
collapsing text in, 110
demoting text in, 108
drag and dropping text
in, 107
expanding text in, 111
formatting text in,
112-114
moving text in, 106
promoting text in, 109
replacing text in, 105
PowerPoint, starting, 3
PowerPoint command
(Programs menu), 3

presentations
color schemes,
changing, 76
charts, *see* charts
creating
AutoContent Wizard,
4-15
templates, 159-162
exiting, 18
fonts, *see* text, fonts, 52
graphs, *see* graphs
navigating, 9
opening, 15
organization charts, *see*
organization charts
packing, 132-136
previewing, 119-120
printing, 115
saving, 14
slide master, editing,
65-66
slides, *see* slide shows;
slides
starting, 16-17
stopping, 129
styles checker, 50-51
text
deselcting, 8
typing, 8
types of, 6
views, *see* views
previewing presentations,
119-120
Print command
(File menu), 88, 115
Print dialog box, 116, 118
printers, configura-
tions, 115
printing
handouts, 88
notes, 88
presentations, 115,
119-120
print job
canceling, 118
settings, 118
printers, setting, 116-117
slides, 118
Programs menu
commands, Power-
Point, 3
promoting text in
placeholders, 109

Q-R

quitting, *see* exiting
presentations

raster graphics, 117
Recolorcommand
(Tools menu), 173
removing
slides, 11
indents, text, 109
legends from graphs, 36
Replace command
(Edit menu), 62
replacing text, 41,
62-63, 105
resolution, defined, 117
restoring
graphs, 37
legends, 36
rotating graphs, 29
Row/Column command
(Data menu), 22
Rows
graphs, 32
tables
adding, 150
height, 155
ruler
displaying, 143
hiding, 143
Ruler command
(Tools menu), 143

S

Save As command
(File menu), 166
Save command
(File menu), 14
saving
files, 14
presentations, 14
slide master, 166
timing of slide
shows, 128
Select command
(Edit menu), 104
selecting
organization chart
parts, 104
slides, 17
text, 39
Selection command
(Edit menu), 180-181

Send to Genigraphics command (File menu), 120
setting options, 145
shading
  slides
    adding, 68-69
    selecting, 69
    texture, 71
  tables, 157-158
Shadow command (Boxes menu), 97
shadows
  adding, 187
  organization charts, 96-97
Shortcut bar (Microsoft Office), 3
Shortcut menu, displaying, 44
sizing
  fonts, 53
  graphs, 35
  notes pages, 79
  slides, 73
  toolbars, floating toolbars, 139
Slide Color Scheme command (Format menu), 30, 76, 163-164
Slide Layout command (Format menu), 67
slide master
  changing, 165
  editing, 65-66
  saving, 166
Slide Master command (View menu), 165
Slide Setup command (File menu), 73
slide shows, creating builds, 123
Slide Show command (View menu), 127
slide shows
  annotating slides during presentation, 130
  copying slides from other presentations, 121
  creating builds
    graphics, 124
    text, 124-125
    text builds, 122-123
  creating hidden slides, 131
  displaying hidden slides, 131

ending, 132
running
  continuously, 129
  running, manulally, 127
  setting timing, 128
spelling check
  AutoCorrect, 48-49
  spell checker, 47
timing, saving, 128
transitions, 126
viewing, 127
see also slides, 127
Slide Sorter command (View menu), 13
Slide Transition command (Tools menu), 126
slides
  adding to presentations, 11
  annotating during presentation, 130
  background
    clip art, 72
    mutes, 162
    patterns, 70
    shading, 68-69
    texture, 71
  build
    graphics, 123-125
    text, 122-125
  charts, organization charts, 89-96, *see also* organization charts
  clipart, 167-168, 170
    AutoClipArt, 170
    cropping, 174
    replacing, 169
  color, 162
  color scheme, changing, 76, 163-164
  copying from other presentations, 121
  dates, adding, 75
  deleting, 11
  entering text, 7
  fonts, changing, 52
  footers, 74
  formats, changing, 73
  graphs, adding, 19-20
  guides
    displaying, 144
    moving, 144
  handouts, *see* handouts
  inserting into presentations, 10

layout, changing, 67
Media Player
  selecting clips, 180-181
  volume, 182
movies, 175-176
moving, 9, 13
music clips, 179-180
notes, *see* notes
numbers, adding, 75
orientation, 73
outlines, text, 105-114
printing
  hidden slides, 118
  settings, 118
removing, 11
scaling, 118
selecting, 17
sizing, 73
slide master
  changing, 165
  editing, 65-66
  saving, 166
sorting, 13
sound clips, 177-178
tables, *see* tables
text
  animating, 77-78
  applying multiple attributes, 55
  copying, 44
  cutting, 43
  drag and drop, 46
  editing, 40-41
  finding, 61
  font styles, 54
  formatting in headers/footers, 86
  inserting into existing text, 42
  line spacing, 57
  paragraph alignment, 56
  paragraph bullets, 59-60
  paragraph spacing, 58
  pasting, 45
  replacing, 8, 62-63
  selecting, 39
  sizing fonts, 53
  transitions, 126
undoing deletions, 11
writing on, 130
sorting slides, 13

sound clips, WAV format,
177-178
sounds
in slides, 177-178
Media Player
selecting clips, 180-181
volume, 182
Spell checker, adding
names, 47
Spelling command
(Tools menu), 47
spreadsheet tables, 22-23
starting
PowerPoint, 3
presentations, 16-17
stopping
presentations, 129
slide shows, 132
structure, organization
charts
adding levels, 100
reporting structure,
101-102
Style Checker command
(Tools menu), 50
styles
organization charts, 103
presentations, handling
errors, 50-51
text, outlines, 112-114
switching views,
presentations, 12

T

Table AutoFormat command
(Table menu), 152
Table menu commands,
152, 155
tables
adding to slides, 147-149
cells
editing data, 151
entering data, 150
columns, width, 155
formatting
AutoFormat, 152-153
borders, 156
cells, 155
shading, 157-158
text, 154

rows
adding, 150
height, 155
spreadsheet tables, 22-23
templates
Design templates
creating, 161-162
creating presentations,
159-160
opening, 161-162
text
alignment
line spacing, 57
paragraphs, 56
animating, 77-78
deselecting, 8
editing
deleting characters, 40
replacing existing
text, 41
entering into place-
holders, 7
finding, 61
fonts
applying multiple
attributes, 55
applying styles, 54
changing, 52
sizing, 53
footers, creating, 74
formatting in headers/
footers, 86
graphs
font, 33
formatting, 33
headers, creating, 74
indenting, 108-109
inserting into existing
text, 42
organization charts
color, 99
fonts, 98
outlines, *see* outlines
paragraphs
bullets, 59-60
spacing, 58
replacing, 62-63
replacing in slides, 8
selecting, 39
slides, *see* slides
tables, formatting , 154
typing, 8

Text menu commands, 98-99
timing slide shows
saving, 128
setting, 128
tips, hiding, 3
toolbars
adding commands, 141
Animation, displaying, 123
buttons, customizing, 142
creating, custom toolbars,
140-141
displaying, 137
floating, sizing, 139
hiding, 137
moving, 138
Toolbars command
(View menu), 140
Tools menu commands, *see*
individual commands
transitions (slides), 126
typing text, 8

U-V

Undo command
(Edit menu), 11
undoing deletions
(slides), 11

vector graphics, 117
View menu commands, *see*
individual commands
View tab, 146
viewing slide shows, 127
views, presentations
Outline, 106
Slide View, 12
switching, 12
Zoom view, 84

W-Z

WAV format, 177-178
Windows
Clipboard, 43
Datasheet window, 21
wizards
AutoContent, 5-15
AutoContent Wizard,
creating presen-
tations, 4
Pack and Go, 132-136
writing on slides, 130
Zoom view, 84